The Happiness Trap

How to Stop Struggling and Start Living

RUSS HARRIS

Foreword by Steven Hayes, PhD

Trumpeter
Boulder
2008

Trumpeter Books
An imprint of Shambhala Publications, Inc.
2129 13th Street
Boulder, Colorado 80302
www.shambhala.com

Published by arrangement with Exisle Publishing Ltd,
Wollombi, Australia

The cases mentioned in this book are all based on real people, but,
to protect privacy, key identifying details have been changed.

29 28 27 26 25 24 23 22

Printed in the United States of America

∞ This edition is printed on acid-free paper that meets the American
National Standards Institute Z39.48 Standard.
♲ This book is printed on 30% postconsumer recycled paper.
For more information please visit www.shambhala.com.

Trumpeter Books is distributed worldwide
by Penguin Random House, Inc., and its subsidiaries.

Interior design and composition: Greta D. Sibley & Associates

Library of Congress Cataloging-in-Publication Data
Harris, Russ, 1966–
The happiness trap: how to stop struggling and start living /
Russ Harris; foreword by Steven Hayes.
p. cm.
Includes index.
ISBN 978-1-59030-584-3 (pbk.: alk. paper)
1. Happiness. I. Title.
BF575.H27H375 2008
158.1—dc22
2007042105

The Happiness Trap

*To my mother and father, for four decades of love, support,
inspiration, and encouragement. And to my wife Carmel,
whose love, wisdom, and generosity have enriched my
life and opened my heart in ways I would
never have dreamed possible.*

Contents

Contents

PART THREE

Creating a Life Worth Living

Foreword

There is a tremendous irony in happiness. It comes from
a root word meaning "by chance" or "an occurrence," which in a positive sense connotes a sense of newness, wonder, and appreciation of
chance occurrences. The irony is that people not only seek it, they try
to hold on to it—especially to avoid any sense of "unhappiness." Unfortunately, these very control efforts can become heavy, planned, closed,
rigid, and fixed.

Happiness is not just a matter of feeling good. If it were, drug abusers
would be the happiest people on the planet. Indeed, feeling good can
be a very unhappy pursuit. It is not by accident that drug users call their
methods of doing so a "fix"—because they are chemically trying to hold
something in place. Like a butterfly pinned to a table, however, happiness dies unless it is held lightly. Drug abusers are not the only ones. In
the name of producing an emotional result we call happiness, most of
us tend to engage in behavior that is the exact opposite and then feel
awful and inadequate with the inevitable result. Until we wise up, we
are all generally trying to get a "fix" on happiness.

This book is based on Acceptance and Commitment Therapy (ACT),
which is an empirically supported approach that takes a new and unexpected tack in dealing with the issue of happiness and life satisfaction.
Instead of teaching new techniques to pursue happiness, ACT teaches
ways to undermine struggle, avoidance, and loss of the moment. Russ
Harris has very carefully and creatively presented this approach in an accessible way. In thirty-three bite-sized chapters he systematically explores

how we get into the "Happiness Trap" and how mindfulness, acceptance, cognitive defusion, and values can release us from it.

The joyful message in these pages is that there is no reason to continue to wait for life to start. That waiting game can end. Now. Like a lion placed in a paper cage, human beings are generally most trapped by the illusions of their own mind. But despite the appearance the cage is not really a barrier that can contain the human spirit. There is another way forward, and with this book Dr. Harris shines a powerful and loving beacon forward into the night, lighting that path.

Enjoy the journey. You are in excellent hands.

> —Steven C. Hayes, PhD
> Originator of ACT
> University of Nevada

Introduction

I Just Want to Be Happy!

Just suppose for a moment that almost everything you believed about finding happiness turned out to be inaccurate, misleading, or false. And suppose that those very beliefs were making you miserable. What if your very efforts to find happiness were actually preventing you from achieving it? And what if almost everyone you knew turned out to be in the same boat—including all those psychologists, psychiatrists, and self-help gurus who claim to have all the answers?

I'm not posing these questions just to grab your attention. This book is based on a growing body of scientific research that suggests we are all caught in a powerful psychological trap. We lead our lives ruled by many unhelpful and inaccurate beliefs about happiness—ideas widely accepted because "everyone knows they are true." These beliefs seem to make good sense—that's why you encounter them in nearly every self-help book you ever read. But unfortunately, these misleading ideas create a vicious cycle in which the more we try to find happiness, the more we suffer. And this psychological trap is so well hidden, we don't even have a clue that we're caught in it.

That's the bad news.

The good news is there's hope. You can learn how to recognize the "happiness trap" and, more importantly, you can learn how to escape. And this book will give you the skills and knowledge to do so. It's based on a revolutionary new development in human psychology, a powerful model for change known as Acceptance and Commitment Therapy, or ACT.

ACT (pronounced like the word "act") was developed in the United States by psychologist Steven Hayes and his colleagues, Kelly Wilson and Kirk Strosahl. ACT has been astoundingly effective in helping people with a wide range of problems from depression and anxiety to chronic pain and even drug addiction. For example, in one remarkable study, psychologists Patty Bach and Steven Hayes used ACT with patients suffering from chronic schizophrenia and found that only four hours of therapy were sufficient to reduce hospital readmission rates by half! ACT has also proved highly effective for the less dramatic problems that millions of us encounter, such as quitting smoking and reducing stress in the workplace. Unlike the vast majority of other therapies, ACT has a firm basis in scientific research and because of this, it is rapidly growing in popularity among psychologists all around the world.

The aim of ACT is to help you live a rich, full, and meaningful life while effectively handling the pain that inevitably comes your way. ACT achieves this through the use of six powerful principles, which will enable you to develop a life-enhancing ability known as "psychological flexibility."

Is Happiness Normal?

In the western world we now have a higher standard of living than humans have ever known before. We have better medical treatment, better food, better housing conditions, better sanitation, more money, more welfare services, and more access to education, justice, travel, entertainment, and career opportunities. Indeed, today's middle class lives better than did the royalty of not so long ago. And yet humans today don't seem very happy. The self-help sections of bookstores are packed with books on depression, anxiety, stress, relationship problems, addiction, and more. Meanwhile, on the television and radio the "experts" bombard us daily with advice on how to improve our lives. The number of psychologists, psychiatrists, marriage and family counselors, social workers, and "life coaches" is increasing every year. Yet despite all this help and advice, human unhappiness does not seem to be diminishing but growing by leaps and bounds! Isn't there something wrong with this picture?

The statistics are staggering: In any given year almost 30 percent of the adult population will suffer from a recognized psychological disorder. The World Health Organization estimates that depression is currently the fourth biggest, costliest, and most debilitating disease in the world and by the year 2020, it will be the second biggest. In any given week, one-tenth of the adult population is suffering from clinical depression, and one in five people will suffer from it at some point in their lifetime. Furthermore, one in four adults, at some stage in their life, will suffer from drug or alcohol addiction, which is why there are now over twenty million alcoholics in the United States alone.

But more startling and more sobering than all those statistics is that almost one in two people will go through a stage in life when they seriously consider suicide and will struggle with it for a period of two weeks or more. Scarier still, one in ten people will at some point actually attempt to kill themselves.

Think about those numbers for a moment. Think of your friends, family, and coworkers. Almost half of them will at some point be so overwhelmed by misery that they seriously contemplate suicide. One in ten will actually go on to attempt it. Clearly, lasting happiness is not normal!

Why Is It So Difficult to Be Happy?

To answer this question, let's take a journey back in time. The modern human mind, with its amazing ability to analyze, plan, create, and communicate has largely evolved over the last hundred thousand years, since our species, *Homo sapiens*, first appeared on the planet. But our minds did not evolve to make us "feel good" so we could tell jokes, write poems, or say "I love you." Our minds evolved to help us survive in a world fraught with danger.

Imagine that you're an early human hunter-gatherer. What are your essential needs in order to survive and reproduce? There are four of them: food, water, shelter, and sex. But none of these things matter if you're dead. So the number one priority of the primitive human mind was to look out for anything that might harm you—and avoid it. The primitive mind was basically a "Don't get killed" device, and it proved enormously useful. The better our ancestors became at anticipating and avoiding danger, the longer they lived and the more children they had.

So with each generation the human mind became increasingly skilled at predicting and avoiding danger. And now, after one hundred thousand years of evolution, the modern mind is constantly on the lookout, assessing and judging everything we encounter: Is this good or bad? Safe or dangerous? Harmful or helpful? These days, though, it's not saber-toothed tigers or woolly mammoths that our mind warns us about. Instead it's losing our job, being rejected, getting a speeding ticket, embarrassing ourselves in public, getting cancer, or a million and one other common worries. As a result we spend a lot of time worrying about things that, more often than not, never happen.

Another essential for the survival of any early human is to belong to a group. If your clan boots you out, it won't be long before the wolves find you. So how does the mind protect you from rejection by the group? By comparing you with other members of the clan: Am I fitting in? Am I doing the right thing? Am I contributing enough? Am I as good as the others? Am I doing anything that might get me rejected?

Sound familiar? Our modern-day minds are continually warning us of rejection and comparing us to the rest of society. No wonder we spend so much energy worrying whether people will like us! No wonder we're always looking for ways to improve ourselves or putting ourselves down because we don't "measure up." A hundred thousand years ago we had only the few members of our immediate clan to compare ourselves with. But these days we only need to glance at a newspaper, magazine, or television to instantly find a whole host of people who are smarter, richer, slimmer, sexier, more famous, more powerful, or more successful than we are. When we compare ourselves to these glamorous media creations, we feel inferior or disappointed with our lives. To make matters worse, our minds are now so sophisticated they can conjure up a fantasy image of the person we'd ideally like to be—and then we compare ourselves to that! What chance have we got? We will always end up feeling not good enough.

Now, for any Stone Age person with ambition, the general rule for success is: get more and get better. The better your weapons, the more food you can kill. The larger your food stores, the greater your chances for survival in times of scarcity. The better your shelter, the safer you are from weather and wild animals. The more children you have, the greater the chance that some will survive into adulthood. No surprise then that our modern mind continually looks for "more and better": more money, a better job, more status, a better body, more love, a better partner. And if we succeed, if we actually do get more money or a better car or a better-looking body, then we're satisfied—for a while. But sooner or later (and usually sooner), we end up wanting more.

Thus, evolution has shaped our brains so that we are hardwired to suffer psychologically: to compare, evaluate, and criticize ourselves, to focus on what we're lacking, to rapidly become dissatisfied with what we have, and to imagine all sorts of frightening scenarios, most of which will never happen. No wonder humans find it hard to be happy!

What Exactly Is "Happiness"?

We all want it. We all crave it. We all strive for it. Even the Dalai Lama has said: "The very purpose of life is to seek happiness." But what exactly is it?

The word "happiness" has two very different meanings. The common meaning of the word is "feeling good." In other words, feeling a sense of pleasure, gladness, or gratification. We all enjoy these feelings, so it's no surprise that we chase them. However, like all human emotions, feelings of happiness don't last. No matter how hard we try to hold on to them, they slip away every time. And as we shall see, a life spent in pursuit of those good feelings is, in the long term, deeply unsatisfying. In fact, the harder we chase after pleasurable feelings, the more we are likely to suffer from anxiety and depression.

The other far less common meaning of happiness is "living a rich, full, and meaningful life." When we take action on the things that truly matter deep in our hearts, move in directions that we consider valuable and worthy, clarify what we stand for in life and act accordingly, then our lives become rich and full and meaningful, and we experience a powerful sense of vitality. This is not some fleeting feeling—it is a profound sense of a life well lived. And although such a life will undoubtedly give us many pleasurable feelings, it will also give us uncomfortable ones, such as sadness, fear, and anger. This is only to be expected. If we live a full life, we will feel the full range of human emotions.

In this book, as you've probably guessed by now, we are far more interested in this second meaning of happiness than in the first. Of course, we all enjoy feeling good, and we should certainly make the most of pleasant feelings when they appear. But if we try to have them all the time, we are doomed to failure.

The reality is, life involves pain. There's no getting away from it. As human beings we are all faced with the fact that sooner or later we will grow infirm, get sick, and die. Sooner or later we all will lose valued relationships through rejection, separation, or death. Sooner or later we all will come face to face with crisis, disappointment, and failure. This means that in one form or another, we are all going to experience painful thoughts and feelings.

The good news is that, although we can't avoid such pain, we can learn to handle it much better—to make room for it, reduce its impact, and create a life worth living despite it. This book will show you how to do it. There are three parts to this process. In part 1 you will learn how you create and get stuck in the happiness trap. This is an essential first step, so please don't skip it. You can't escape the trap if you don't know how it works. In part 2, rather than trying to avoid or eliminate painful thoughts and feelings, you will learn how to make room for them and experience them in a new way that will reduce their impact, drain away their power, and dramatically decrease their influence over your life. Finally, in part 3, instead of chasing happy thoughts and feelings, you will focus on creating a rich and meaningful life. This will give rise to a sense of vitality and fulfillment that is both deeply satisfying and long lasting.

The Journey Ahead

This book is like a trip through a foreign country: much will seem strange and new. Other things will seem familiar yet somehow subtly different. At times you may feel challenged or confronted, at other times excited or amused. Take your time on this journey. Instead of rushing ahead, savor it fully. Stop when you find something stimulating or unusual. Explore it in depth and learn as much as you can. To create a life worth living is a major undertaking, so please take the time to appreciate it.

PART ONE

How You Set the Happiness Trap

1
Fairy Tales

What's the last line of every fairy tale? You got it: "... and they lived happily every after." And it's not just fairy tales that have happy endings. How about Hollywood movies? Don't they nearly always have some sort of feel-good ending where good triumphs over evil, love conquers all, and the hero defeats the bad guy? And doesn't the same hold true for most popular novels and television programs? We love happy endings because society tells us that's how life should be: all joy and fun, peace and contentment, living happily ever after. But does that sound realistic? Does it fit in with your experience of life? This is one of four major myths that make up the basic blueprint for the happiness trap. Let's take a look at these myths, one by one.

Myth 1: Happiness Is the Natural State for All Human Beings

Our culture insists that humans are naturally happy. But the statistics quoted in the introduction clearly disprove this. Remember, one in ten adults will attempt suicide, and one in five will suffer from depression. What's more, the statistical probability that you will suffer from a psychiatric disorder at some stage in your life is almost 30 percent!

And when you add in all the misery caused by problems that are not classified as psychiatric disorders—loneliness, divorce, work stress, midlife crisis, relationship issues, social isolation, prejudice, and lack of meaning or purpose—you start to get some idea of just how rare true happiness really is. Unfortunately, many people walk around with the belief that everyone else is happy except them. And—you guessed it—this belief creates even more unhappiness.

Myth 2: If You're Not Happy, You're Defective

Following logically from Myth 1, Western society assumes that mental suffering is abnormal. It is seen as a weakness or illness, a product of a mind that is somehow faulty or defective. This means that when we do inevitably experience painful thoughts and feelings, we often criticize ourselves for being weak or stupid.

Acceptance and Commitment Therapy is based on a dramatically different assumption: the normal thinking processes of a healthy human mind will naturally lead to psychological suffering. You're not defective; your mind's just doing what it evolved to do. Fortunately, ACT will teach you to handle your mind more effectively, in ways which can dramatically improve your life.

Myth 3: To Create a Better Life, We Must Get Rid of Negative Feelings

We live in a feel-good society, a culture thoroughly obsessed with finding happiness. And what does that society tell us to do? To eliminate "negative" feelings and accumulate "positive" ones in their place. It's a nice theory, and on the surface it seems to make sense. After all, who wants to have unpleasant feelings? But here's the catch: the things we generally value most in life bring with them a whole range of feelings, both pleasant and unpleasant. For example, in an intimate long-term relationship, although you will experience wonderful feelings such as love and joy, you will also inevitably experience disappointment and frustration. There is no such thing as the perfect partner, and sooner or later conflicts of interest will arise.

The same holds true for just about every meaningful project we embark on. Although they often bring feelings of excitement and enthusiasm, they also generally bring stress, fear, and anxiety. So if you believe Myth 3, you're in big trouble because it's pretty well impossible to create a better life if you're not prepared to have some uncomfortable feelings. However, in part 2 of this book you will learn how to handle such feelings altogether differently, to experience them in such a way that they have much less impact on you.

Myth 4: You Should Be Able to Control What You Think and Feel

The fact is, we have much less control over our thoughts and feelings than we would like. It's not that we have no control; it's just that we have much less than the "experts" would have us believe. However, we do have a huge amount of control over our actions. And it's through taking action that we create a rich, full, and meaningful life.

The overwhelming majority of self-help programs subscribe to Myth 4. The basic claim is: if you challenge your negative thoughts or images and, instead, repeatedly fill your head with positive thoughts and images, you will find happiness. If only life were that simple!

I'm willing to bet that you've already tried countless times to think more positively about things, and yet those negative thoughts keep coming back, don't they? As we saw in the introduction, our minds have evolved over a hundred thousand years to think the way they do, so it's not likely that a few positive thoughts will change them much. It's not that these techniques have no effect; they can often make you feel better temporarily. But they will not get rid of negative thoughts over the long term.

The same holds true for "negative" feelings such as anger, fear, sadness, insecurity, and guilt. There are multitudes of psychological strategies to "get rid of" such feelings. But you've undoubtedly discovered that even if they go away, after awhile they're back. And then they go away again. And then they come back again. And so on and so on. The likelihood is, if you're like most other humans on the planet, you've already spent a lot of time and effort trying to have "good" feelings instead of "bad" ones, and you've probably found that as long as you're not too distressed, you can, to some degree, pull it off. But you've probably also discovered that as your level of distress increases, your ability to control your feelings progressively lessens. Sadly, Myth 4 is so widely believed that we tend to feel inadequate when our attempts to control our thoughts and feelings fail.

These four powerful myths provide the basic blueprint for the happiness trap. They set us up for a struggle we can never win: the struggle against our own human nature. It is this struggle that builds the trap. In the next chapter we will look at this struggle in detail, but first let's consider why these myths are so entrenched in our culture.

The Illusion of Control

The human mind has given us an enormous advantage as a species. It enables us to make plans, invent things, coordinate actions, analyze problems, share knowledge, learn from our experiences, and imagine new futures. The clothes on your body, the chair beneath you, the roof over your head, the book in your hands—none of these things would exist but for the ingenuity of the human mind. The mind enables us to shape the world around us and conform it to our wishes, to provide ourselves with warmth, shelter, food, water, protection, sanitation, and medicine. Not surprisingly, this amazing ability to control our environment gives us high expectations of control in other arenas as well.

Now, in the material world, control strategies generally work well. If we don't like something, we figure out how to avoid it or get rid of it, and then we do so. A wolf outside your door? Get rid of it! Throw rocks at it, or spears, or shoot it. Snow, rain, or hail? Well you can't get rid of those things, but you can avoid them by hiding in a cave or building a shelter. Dry, arid soil? You can get rid of it by irrigation and fertilization, or you can avoid it by moving to fertile ground.

But how much control do we have in our internal world; the world of thoughts, memories, emotions, urges, and sensations? Can we simply avoid or get rid of the ones we don't like? Well, let's see. Here's a little experiment. As you keep reading this paragraph, try not to think about your favorite flavor of ice cream. Don't think about the color or the texture. Don't think about how it tastes on a hot summer day. Don't think about how good it feels as it melts inside your mouth.

How'd you do? Exactly! You couldn't stop thinking about ice cream.

Now here's another little experiment. Bring to mind your earliest childhood memory. Get a picture of it in your head. Got it? Good. Now delete it. Totally obliterate that memory so it can never come back to you again.

How did it go? (If you think you succeeded, just check again and see if you can still remember it.)

Next, tune in to your left leg and notice how it feels. Feeling it? Good. Now make it go completely numb—so numb, that we could cut it off with a hacksaw and you wouldn't feel a thing.

Did you succeed?

Okay, now here's another little thought experiment. Imagine someone puts a loaded gun to your head and tells you that you must not feel afraid; that if you feel even the slightest trace of anxiety, then they will shoot you. Could you stop yourself feeling anxious in that situation, even though your life depends on it? (Sure you could *pretend* to be calm, but could you truly *feel* calm?)

Now, one last experiment. Stare at the star below, then see if you can stop yourself from thinking for two minutes. That's all you have to do. For two minutes, prevent any thoughts whatsoever from coming into your mind—especially any thoughts about the star!

Hopefully by now you're getting the point that thoughts, feelings, sensations, and memories are just not that easy to control. It's not that you don't have *any* control over these things; it's just that you have much less control than you thought. Let's face it, if these things were that easy to control, wouldn't we all just live in perpetual bliss?

How We Learn about Control

From a young age, we are taught that we should be able to control our feelings. When you were growing up, you probably heard a number of expressions like, "Don't cry," "Don't be so gloomy," "Stop feeling sorry for yourself," "There's nothing to be afraid of."

With words such as these, the adults around us sent out the message again and again that we ought to be able to control our feelings. And certainly it appeared to us as if they controlled theirs. But what was going on behind closed doors? In all likelihood, many of those adults weren't coping too well with their own painful feelings. They may have been drinking too much, taking tranquilizers, crying themselves to sleep every night, having affairs, throwing themselves into their work, or suffering in silence while slowly developing stomach ulcers. However they were coping, they probably didn't share those experiences with you.

And on those rare occasions when you did get to witness their loss of control, they probably never said anything like, "Okay, these tears are because I'm feeling something called sadness. It's a normal feeling, and you can learn how to handle it effectively." But then, that's not too surprising; they couldn't show you how to handle your emotions because they didn't know how to handle theirs!

The idea that you should be able to control your feelings was undoubtedly reinforced in your school years. For example, kids who cried at school were probably teased for being "crybabies" or "sissies" — especially if they were boys. Then, as you grew older, you probably heard phrases (or even used them yourself) such as, "Get over it!" "Shit happens!" "Move on!" "Chill out!" "Don't be a chicken!" "Snap out of it!" and so on.

These phrases imply that you should be able to turn your feelings on and off at will, like flicking a switch. And why is this myth so compelling? Because the people around us seem, on the surface, to be happy. They seem to be in control of their thoughts and feelings. But "seem" is the key word here. The fact is that most people are not open or honest about the struggle they go through with their own thoughts and feelings. They "put on a brave face" and "keep a stiff upper lip." They are like the proverbial clown crying on the inside; the bright face paint and chirpy antics are all we see. I commonly hear my clients say things like, "If my friends/family/colleagues could hear me now, they'd never believe it. Everyone thinks I'm so strong/confident/happy/independent."

Penny, a thirty-year-old receptionist, came to see me six months after the birth of her first child. She was feeling tired and anxious and full of self-doubt about her mothering skills. At times she felt incompetent or inadequate and just wanted to run away from all the responsibility. At other times she felt exhausted and miserable and wondered if having a child had been a huge mistake. On top of that, she felt guilty for even having such thoughts! Although Penny attended regular mothers' group meetings, she kept her problems a secret. The other mothers all seemed so confident, she feared that if she told them how she was feeling, they would look down on her. When Penny eventually plucked up the courage to share her experiences with the other women, her admission broke a conspiracy of silence. The other mothers had all been feeling the same way to one degree or another, but they'd all been putting on the same act of bravado, hiding their true feelings for fear of disapproval or rejection. There was a huge sense of relief and bonding as these women opened up and got honest with one another.

To make a gross generalization, men are much worse than women at admitting their deepest concerns because men are taught to be stoic, to bottle up their feelings and hide them. After all, big boys don't cry. In contrast, women learn to share and discuss their feelings from a young age. Nonetheless, many women are reluctant to tell even their closest friends that they are feeling depressed or anxious or not coping in some way, for fear of being judged weak or silly. Our silence about what we are really feeling and the false front we put on for the people around us simply add to the powerful illusion of control.

So the question is: How much have you been influenced by all these control myths? The questionnaire on the following pages will help you find out.

QUESTIONNAIRE

Control of Thoughts and Feelings

This questionnaire has been adapted from similar ones developed by Steven Hayes, Frank Bond, and others. When the phrase "negative thoughts and feelings" is used, it refers to a whole range of painful feelings (anger, depression, and anxiety) and painful thoughts (bad memories, disturbing images, and harsh self-judgments). For each pair of statements, please select the one that most accurately fits how you feel. The answer you choose doesn't have to be absolutely 100 percent true for you all the time; just pick the answer which seems to be more representative of your general attitude. (If you don't want to write in this book, you can download a free copy of this questionnaire from the resources page on www.thehappinesstrap.com.)

1a. I must have good control of my feelings in order to be successful in life.
1b. It is unnecessary for me to control my feelings in order to be successful in life.

2a. Anxiety is bad.
2b. Anxiety is neither good nor bad. It is merely an uncomfortable feeling.

3a. Negative thoughts and feelings will harm you if you don't control or get rid of them.
3b. Negative thoughts and feelings won't harm you even if they feel unpleasant.

4a. I'm afraid of some of my strong feelings.
4b. I'm not afraid of any feelings, no matter how strong.

5a. In order for me to do something important, I have to get rid of all my doubts.
5b. I can do something important, even when doubts are present.

6a. When negative thoughts and feelings arise, it's important to reduce or get rid of them as quickly as possible.
6b. Trying to reduce or get rid of negative thoughts and feelings frequently causes problems. If I simply allow them to be, then they will change as a natural part of living.

(7a.) The best method of managing negative thoughts and feelings is to analyze them; then utilize that knowledge to get rid of them.

7b. The best method of managing negative thoughts and feelings is to acknowledge their presence and let them be, without having to analyze or judge them.

(8a.) I will become "happy" and "healthy" by improving my ability to avoid, reduce, or get rid of negative thoughts and feelings.

8b. I will become "happy" and "healthy" by allowing negative thoughts and feelings to come and go of their own accord and learning to live effectively when they are present.

9a. If I can't suppress or get rid of a negative emotional reaction, it's a sign of personal failure or weakness.

(9b.) The need to control or get rid of a negative emotional reaction is a problem in itself.

10a. Having negative thoughts and feelings is an indication that I'm psychologically unhealthy or I've got problems.

(10b.) Having negative thoughts and feelings means I'm a normal human being.

11a. People who are in control of their lives can generally control how they feel.

(11b.) People who are in contol of their lives do not need to control their feelings.

12a. It is not okay to feel anxious, and I try hard to avoid it.

(12b.) I don't like anxiety, but it's okay to feel it.

13a. Negative thoughts and feelings are a sign that there is something wrong with my life.

(13b.) Negative thoughts and feelings are an inevitable part of life for everyone.

(14a.) I have to feel good before I can do something that's important and challenging.

14b. I can do something that's important and challenging even if I'm feeling anxious or depressed.

(15a.) I try to suppress thoughts and feelings that I don't like by just not thinking about them.

15b. I don't try to suppress thoughts and feelings that I don't like. I just let them come and go of their own accord.

To score your test, count the number of times you selected option "a" or "b." (Please keep a record of your score. At the end of this book, I'll ask you to come back and do this test again.)

The more times you selected option "a," the greater the likelihood that control issues are creating significant suffering in your life. How so? That's the subject of the next chapter.

2

Vicious Cycles

Michelle has tears streaming down her eyes. "What's wrong with me?" she asks. "I have a great husband, great kids, a great job, a lovely home. I'm fit, healthy, well-off. So why aren't I happy?" It's a good question. Michelle seems to have everything she wants in life, so what's going wrong? We'll come back to Michelle later in this chapter, but for now let's take a look at what's happening in your life.

Presumably, if you're reading this book, your life could work better than it does right now. Maybe your relationship is in trouble, or you're lonely or heartbroken. Maybe you hate your job or perhaps you've lost it. Maybe your health is deteriorating. Maybe someone you love has died or rejected you or moved far away. Maybe you have low self-esteem or no self-confidence. Maybe you have an addiction or financial problems or legal difficulties. Maybe you're suffering from depression, anxiety, or "burnout." Or maybe you just feel stuck or disillusioned.

Whatever the problem is, it undoubtedly gives rise to unpleasant thoughts and feelings—and you've probably spent a lot of time and effort trying to escape them or blot them out. But suppose those attempts to get rid of your bad thoughts and feelings are actually making your life worse? In ACT we have a saying for this: "The solution is the problem!"

How Does a Solution Become a Problem?

What do you do when you have an itch? You scratch it, right? And usually this works so well you don't even think about it: scratch the itch and it goes away. Problem solved. But suppose one day you develop a patch of eczema (red, irritated skin). The skin is very itchy, so naturally you scratch it. However, with this condition, the skin cells are highly sensitive, and when you scratch them, they release chemicals called histamines, which lead to further irritation and inflammation. So very soon the itch returns—but with a greater intensity than before. And, of course, if you scratch it again, it gets even worse!

Scratching is a good solution for a fleeting itch in normal, healthy skin. But for a persistent itch in abnormal skin, scratching is harmful. The "solution" becomes part of the problem. This is commonly known as a "vicious cycle." And in the world of human emotions, vicious cycles are common. Here are a few examples:

- Joseph fears rejection, so he feels very anxious in social situations. He doesn't want those feelings of anxiety, so he avoids socializing whenever possible. He doesn't accept invitations to parties. He doesn't pursue friendships. He lives alone and stays home every night. This means that on the rare occasion when he does socialize, he's more anxious than ever because he's so out of practice. Furthermore, living alone with no friends or social life just serves to make him feel completely rejected, which is the very thing he fears!

- Yvonne also feels anxious in social situations. She copes with this by drinking heavily. In the short term, alcohol reduces her anxiety. But the next day she feels hungover and tired and she often regrets the money she spent on alcohol or worries about the embarrassing things she did while under the influence. Sure, she escapes anxiety for a little while, but the price she pays is a lot of other unpleasant feelings over the long term. And if she ever finds herself in a social situation where she can't drink, her anxiety is greater than ever, because she doesn't have alcohol to rely on.

- There's a lot of built-up tension between Andrew and his wife, Sylvana. Sylvana is angry at Andrew because he works long hours and doesn't spend enough time with her. Andrew doesn't like those feelings of tension in the house, so in order to avoid them, he starts working longer hours. But the more hours he works, the more dissatisfied Sylvana gets, and the tension in their relationship steadily increases.

- Danielle is overweight and hates it, so she eats some chocolate to cheer herself up. For a few moments, she feels better. But then she thinks about all the calories she's just consumed and how that will add to her weight, and she ends up feeling more miserable than ever.
- Ahmed is out of shape. He wants to get fit again. He starts working out, but because he's unfit, it's hard work and it feels uncomfortable. He doesn't like the discomfort, so he stops working out. Then his fitness level slides even lower.

You can see that these are all examples of trying to get rid of, avoid, or escape from unpleasant feelings. We call these "control strategies" because they are attempts to directly control how you feel. The table below shows some of the most common control strategies. I've organized them into two main categories: fight strategies and flight strategies. Fight strategies involve fighting with or trying to dominate your unwanted thoughts and feelings. Flight strategies involve running away or hiding from those unwelcome thoughts and feelings.

COMMON CONTROL STRATEGIES

FLIGHT STRATEGIES	FIGHT STRATEGIES
Hiding/Escaping	*Suppression*
You hide away or escape from people, places, situations, or activities that tend to give rise to uncomfortable thoughts or feelings. For example, you drop out of a course or cancel a social event in order to avoid feelings of anxiety.	You try to directly suppress unwanted thoughts and feelings. unwanted thoughts and feelings. You forcefully push unwanted thoughts from your mind, or you push your feelings "deep down inside."

FLIGHT STRATEGIES	FIGHT STRATEGIES
Distraction	*Arguing*
You distract yourself from unwanted thoughts and feelings by focusing on something else. For example, you're feeling bored or anxious, so you smoke a cigarette or eat some ice cream or go shopping. Or you're worried about some important issue at work, so you spend all night watching TV to try to keep your mind off it.	You argue with your own thoughts. For example, if your mind says, "You're a failure," you may argue back, "Oh, no I'm not—just look at everything I've achieved in my work." Alternatively, you may argue against reality, protesting, "It shouldn't be like this!"
Zoning Out/Numbing	*Taking Charge*
You try to cut off from your thoughts and feelings by "zoning out" or making yourself numb, most commonly through the use of medication, drugs, or alcohol. Some people do their zoning out by sleeping excessively or simply by "staring at the walls."	You try to take charge of your thoughts and feelings. For example, you may tell yourself things like, "Snap out of it!" "Stay calm!" or "Cheer up!" Or you try to force yourself to be happy when you're not.
	Self-Bullying
	You try to bully yourself into feeling differently. You call yourself names like "loser" or "idiot." Or you criticize and blame yourself: "Don't be so pathetic! You can handle this. Why are you being such a coward?!"

The Problem with Control

What's the problem with using methods like these to try to control your thoughts and feelings? The answer is, nothing if:

- You use them only in moderation.
- You use them only in situations where they can work.
- Using them doesn't stop you from doing the things you value.

If you're not too distressed or upset—if you're just dealing with run-of-the-mill, everyday stress—then deliberate attempts to control your thoughts and feelings aren't likely to be a problem. In some situations distraction can be a good way of dealing with unpleasant emotions. If you've just had a fight with your partner and you're feeling hurt and angry, it could be helpful to distract yourself by going for a walk or burying your head in a book until you calm down. And sometimes zoning out can be beneficial. For example, if you're stressed and drained after a grueling day's work, falling asleep on the couch may be just the ticket to help you rejuvenate.

However, control methods become problematic when:

- You use them excessively.
- You use them in situations where they can't work.
- Using them stops you from doing the things you truly value.

Using Control Excessively

To varying degrees, every one of us uses control strategies to get rid of or avoid difficult feelings. In moderation this is no big deal. For instance, when I'm feeling particularly anxious, I sometimes eat a bar of chocolate. This is basically a form of distraction; an attempt to avoid some unpleasant feeling by focusing on something else. But because I only do this in moderation, it's not a major problem in my life. I maintain a healthy weight, and I don't give myself diabetes. However back in my early twenties, it was a different story. Back then I ate a truckload of cookies and chocolates to try to avoid my anxiety (on a bad day I could go through five family-size packages of chocolate chips), and as a result I became seriously overweight and developed high blood pressure. Thus when used excessively, this control strategy had serious consequences.

If you're worried about upcoming exams, you may try to distract yourself from the anxiety by watching television. Now, that's fine if you're only doing it every now and then, but if you do it too much, you'll spend all your evenings watching television and you won't get any studying done. This, in turn, will create more anxiety as your studies lag further and further behind. Therefore, as a method for anxiety control, distraction simply can't work in the long run. And then there's the obvious: dealing with your anxiety in this way prevents you from doing the one thing that would be genuinely helpful: studying.

The same goes for zoning out with alcohol or drugs. Moderate drinking or taking the occasional tranquilizer isn't likely to have serious long-term consequences. But if such control methods become a crutch, it can easily lead to addiction, which then creates all sorts of complications, giving rise to even more painful feelings.

Trying to Use Control in Situations Where It Can't Work

If you love somebody deeply and you lose that relationship—whether through death, rejection, or separation—you will feel pain. That pain is called grief. Grief is a normal emotional reaction to any significant loss, whether a loved one, a job, or a limb. And, once that pain is accepted, it will pass in its own good time.

Unfortunately, many of us refuse to accept grief. We will do anything rather than feel it. We may bury ourselves in work, drink heavily, throw ourselves into a new relationship "on the rebound," or numb ourselves with prescribed medications. But no matter how hard we try to push grief away, deep down inside it's still there. And eventually it will be back.

It's like holding a ball under the water. As long as you keep holding it down, it stays beneath the surface. But eventually your arm gets tired, and the moment you release your grip, the ball leaps straight up out of the water.

Donna was twenty-five years old when her husband and child died in a tragic car crash. Naturally, she felt an explosion of sadness, fear, loneliness, and despair. But Donna could not accept those painful feelings, and she turned to alcohol to push them away. Getting drunk would temporarily soothe her pain, but once she sobered up, her grief returned with a vengeance, and then she'd drink even more to push it away again. By the time Donna came to see me six months later, she was knocking back two bottles of wine a day, as well as taking Valium and sleeping tablets. The single biggest factor in her recovery was her willingness to stop running away from her pain. Only when she opened herself to her feelings and accepted them as a natural part of the grieving process was she able to come to terms with her terrible loss. This enabled her to grieve effectively for her loved ones and channel her energy into building a new life. (Later in the book, we'll look at how she accomplished that.)

When Using Control Stops Us from Doing What We Value

What do you cherish most in life? Health? Work? Family? Friends? Religion? Sports? Nature? It's no surprise that life is richer and more fulfilling when we actively invest our time and energy in the things that are most important or meaningful to us. Yet all too often our attempts to avoid unpleasant feelings get in the way of doing what we truly value.

For example, suppose you are a professional actor and you love your work. Then one day, quite out of the blue, you develop an intense fear of failure just as you are due to appear onstage. So you refuse to go on (a problem commonly known as "stage fright"). Refusing to go onstage may well reduce your fear temporarily, but it also stops you from doing something you truly value.

Or suppose you've just gone through a divorce. Sadness, fear, and anger are all natural reactions, but you don't want to have these unpleasant feelings. So you try to lift your mood by eating junk food, getting drunk, or chain-smoking cigarettes. But what does this do to your health? I've never met anyone who didn't value their health, and yet many people use control strategies that actively damage their physical bodies.

How Much Control Do We Actually Have?

The degree of control we have over our thoughts and feelings depends largely on how intense they are, and what situation we are in — the less intense the feelings and the less stressful the situation, the more control we have. For instance, if we're dealing with typical everyday stress, and we're in a safe, comfortable environment such as our bedroom or a yoga class or the office of a coach or therapist, then a simple relaxation technique can make us feel calmer right away. However, the more intense our thoughts and feelings are and the more stressful the environment we are in, the less effective our attempts at control will be. Just try feeling totally relaxed when you're going for an interview or arguing with your partner or asking someone out on a date, and you'll soon see what I mean. While you can *act* calmly in those situations, you will not *feel* relaxed, no matter how hard you practice your relaxation techniques.

We also have more control over our thoughts and feelings when the things that we're avoiding aren't too important. For example, if you're avoiding cleaning your messy garage or your car, then it's probably fairly easy to take your mind off it. Why? Because in the larger scheme of things, it's simply not that important. If you don't do it, the sun will still rise tomorrow, and you will continue to draw breath. All that will happen is that your garage or car will remain messy. But suppose you suddenly developed a large, suspicious-looking black mole on your arm and you avoid going to the doctor. Would it be easy to take your mind off it? Sure, you could go to a movie, watch television, or surf the Internet, and maybe, for a little while, you could stop thinking about it. But in the long term, you will inevitably start thinking about that mole, because the consequences of not taking action are potentially serious.

So, because many of the things we avoid are not that important, and because many of our negative thoughts and feelings are not that intense, we find that our control strategies can often make us feel better—at least for a little while. Unfortunately, though, this leads us to believe that we have much more control than we actually do. And this false sense of control is only compounded by the myths we encountered in the last chapter.

What Does Control Have to Do with the Happiness Trap?

The happiness trap is built through ineffective control strategies. In order to feel happy, we try hard to control what we're feeling. But these control strategies have three significant costs:

1. They take up a lot of time and energy and are usually ineffective in the long run.

2. We feel silly, defective, or weak-minded because the thoughts/feelings we're trying to get rid of keep coming back.

3. Many strategies that decrease unpleasant feelings in the short term actually lower our quality of life over the long term.

These unwanted outcomes lead to more unpleasant feelings, and thus even more attempts to control them. It's a vicious cycle. Psychologists have a technical term for this inappropriate or excessive use of control strategies: "experiential avoidance." Experiential avoidance means the ongoing attempt to avoid, escape from, or get rid of unwanted thoughts, feelings, and memories—even when doing so is harmful, useless, or costly. (We call this "experiential avoidance" because thoughts, feelings, memories, sensations, etc., are all "private experiences.") Experiential avoidance is a major cause of depression, anxiety, drug and alcohol addiction, eating disorders, and a vast number of other psychological problems.

So here is the happiness trap in a nutshell: to find happiness, we try to avoid or get rid of bad feelings, but the harder we try, the more bad feelings we create. It's important to get a sense of this for yourself, to trust your own experience rather than simply believing what you read. So with this in mind, please complete the following exercise. (You can download a worksheet for this exercise from the resources page on www.thehappinesstrap.com.)

QUESTIONNAIRE

The Costs of Avoidance

First, complete this sentence: "The thoughts/feelings I'd most like to get rid of are . . ."

Next, take a few minutes to write a list of every single thing you've tried in order to avoid or get rid of these unpleasant thoughts or feelings. Try to remember every strategy you have ever used (whether deliberately or by default). Come up with as many examples as possible, such as: avoiding people, places, or situations where the feeling occurs; using drugs, alcohol, or prescription medications; criticizing or chastising yourself; going into denial; blaming others; using visualization, self-hypnosis, or positive affirmations; reading self-help books; seeing a coach or therapist; praying, talking it through with friends; writing in your diary; smoking; eating; sleeping; putting off important changes or decisions; throwing yourself into work/socializing/hobbies/exercise; or telling yourself, "It will pass."

Once you've done that, go through your list and for each item, ask yourself:

1. Did it get rid of my painful thoughts and feelings *in the long term?*
2. What did it cost me in terms of time, energy, money, health, relationships, and vitality?
3. Did it bring me closer to a rich, full, and meaningful life?

Please put the book down and complete this exercise before reading on. Even if you don't write your answers, please spend a good fifteen minutes seriously thinking about this.

If you did this exercise thoroughly, you probably discovered three things:

1. You've invested a lot of time, effort, and energy trying to avoid or get rid of difficult thoughts and feelings.
2. Many of the strategies you've tried made you feel better in the short term, but did not get rid of your painful thoughts and feelings *in the long term.*
3. Many of these strategies have had significant costs in terms of wasted money, wasted time, wasted energy, and negative effects upon your health, vitality, and relationships. In other words, they made you feel good in the short term, but in the long term, they lowered your quality of life.

Feeling a bit dazed, confused, or disturbed? If so . . . good! This is a major paradigm shift, and it challenges many deeply entrenched beliefs. Strong reactions are quite normal.

Of course, if your control strategies have not had significant costs, or if they have brought you closer to the life you want, then they are not problematic and we don't need to focus on them. We are only concerned about control strategies that lower your quality of life in the long run.

"Wait a moment," I hear you say. "Why haven't you talked about things like giving to charity or working diligently or caring for your friends? Isn't giving to others supposed to make people happy?" Good point. However bear in mind that it's not just the things you do that matter; it's also your motivation for doing them. If you're giving to charity to get rid of thoughts that you're selfish, or you're throwing yourself into work to avoid feelings of inadequacy, or you're looking after your friends to counteract fears of rejection, then chances are, you won't get much satisfaction out of those activities. Why not? Because when your primary motivation is the avoidance of unpleasant thoughts and feelings, this drains the joy and vitality from what you are doing. For example, recall the last time you ate something rich and tasty to get rid of feelings of stress, boredom, or anxiety. Chances are, it wasn't all that satisfying. However, did you ever eat that very same food, not to get rid of bad feelings, but purely and simply to enjoy it and appreciate its taste? I bet you found that much more fulfilling.

Great advice about how to improve your life comes at you from all directions: find a meaningful job, do this great workout, get out in nature, take up a hobby, join a club, contribute to charity, learn new skills, have fun with your friends, and so on. And all these activities can be deeply satisfying if you do them because they are genuinely important and meaningful to you. But if these activities are used mainly to escape from unpleasant thoughts and feelings, chances are, they won't be very rewarding. Why not? Because it's hard to enjoy what you're doing while you're trying to escape from something threatening.

So, when you do things because they are truly meaningful to you, because deep in your heart they truly matter to you, those actions would *not* be classified as control strategies. They would be called "values-guided actions" (I'll explain that term later), and they would be expected to *improve* your life in the long term. But if those very same actions are mainly motivated by experiential avoidance—if their primary purpose is to get rid of bad thoughts and feelings—then they *would* be called control strategies (and it would be very surprising if you found them truly fulfilling).

Remember Michelle, who seems to have everything she wants in life and yet she's not happy? Michelle's life is driven by avoiding feelings of unworthiness. She is plagued by thoughts like, "I'm a lousy wife" and "Why am I so inadequate?" and "Nobody likes me," along with all the accompanying feelings of guilt, anxiety, and disappointment.

Michelle works hard to make those thoughts and feelings go away. She pushes herself to excel at her job, frequently working late to accommodate others; she dotes on her husband and kids and caters to their every whim; she tries to please everyone in her life, always putting their needs in front of her own. The toll this takes on her is enormous. And does it get rid of those upsetting thoughts and feelings? You guessed it. By continually putting herself last and working so hard to win others' approval, she merely reinforces her sense of unworthiness. She is truly stuck in the happiness trap.

How Do I Escape the Happiness Trap?

Increasing your self-awareness is the first step. Notice all the little things you do each day to avoid or get rid of unpleasant thoughts and feelings and also notice the consequences.

Keep a journal or spend a few minutes each day reflecting on this. (You can download a simple form for this from the resources page on www.thehappinesstrap.com.) The faster you can recognize when you're stuck in the trap, the faster you can lift yourself out of it. Does this mean you just have to put up with bad feelings and resign yourself to a life of pain and misery? Not at all. In part 2 of this book you will learn a radically different way of handling unwelcome thoughts and feelings. You'll discover how to take away their power so they can't control you and how to reduce their impact so they can't harm you. But don't rush. Before reading on, take a few days. Notice your attempts at control and how they are working for you. Learn to see the trap for what it is. And look forward to the changes soon to come.

PART TWO

Transforming Your Inner World

3

The Six Core Principles of ACT

Acceptance and Commitment Therapy is based upon six core principles that work together to help you develop a life-changing mind-set known as "psychological flexibility." The greater your psychological flexibility, the better you can handle painful thoughts and feelings and the more effectively you can take action to make your life rich and meaningful. As we progress through the book, we will work through these six core principles, one by one, but first let's take a very brief look at all of them.

1. DEFUSION

   Relating to your thoughts in a new way, so they have much less impact and influence over you. As you learn to defuse painful and unpleasant thoughts, they will lose their ability to frighten, disturb, worry, stress, or depress you. And as you learn to defuse unhelpful thoughts, such as self-limiting beliefs and harsh self-criticisms, they will have much less influence over your behavior.

2. EXPANSION

   Making room for unpleasant feelings and sensations instead of trying to suppress them or push them away. As you open up and make space for these feelings, you will find they bother you much less, and they "move on" much more rapidly, instead of "hanging around" and disturbing you. (The official ACT term for this principle is "acceptance." I have changed it because the word "acceptance" has many different meanings and is often misunderstood.)

3. CONNECTION

Connecting fully with whatever is happening right here, right now; focusing on and engaging in whatever you're doing or experiencing. Instead of dwelling on the past or worrying about the future, you are deeply connected with the present moment. (The official ACT phrase is "Contact with the Present Moment." I have changed it purely for brevity.)

4. THE OBSERVING SELF

A powerful aspect of the mind, which has been largely ignored by western psychology until now. As you get to know this part of yourself, you will further transform your relationship with difficult thoughts and feelings.

5. VALUES

Clarifying and connecting with your values is an essential step for making life meaningful. Your values are reflections of what is most important in your heart: what sort of person you want to be, what is significant and meaningful to you, and what you want to stand for in this life. Your values provide direction for your life and motivate you to make important changes.

6. COMMITTED ACTION

A rich and meaningful life is created through taking action. But not just any action. It happens through effective action, guided by and motivated by your values. And in particular, it happens through committed action: action that you take again and again, no matter how many times you fail or go off track.

Mindfulness Skills

The first four principles above are collectively known as "mindfulness skills." Mindfulness is a mental state of awareness, openness, and focus—a state that conveys enormous physical and psychological benefits. Mindfulness has been known about in the East for thousands of years, but until recently, in the West we could only learn about it through following ancient Eastern practices such as yoga, meditation, or tai chi, or religious paths such as Buddhism, Taoism, or Sufism. Unfortunately, these approaches generally take a long time and a lot of intensive practice to get results, and they typically come packaged with a host of beliefs and rituals that do not necessarily fit well with life in a modern secular society. In contrast, ACT is a scientifically based approach, with no religious or spiritual beliefs attached, that teaches mindfulness skills rapidly and effectively—even in the space of a few minutes.

Mindfulness + Values + Action = Psychological Flexibility

As you apply these principles in your life, you will steadily raise your level of psychological flexibility. Psychological flexibility is the ability to adapt to a situation with awareness, openness, and focus and to take effective action, guided by your values. At the time of this writing, this is not a widely known term—but I'm willing to bet it soon will be, because a wealth of research is now showing its considerable benefits in the workplace, in our personal lives, and in the realms of both physical and psychological health.

It's important to remember that while these six basic principles can transform your life in many positive ways, they aren't the Ten Commandments! You don't *have to* use them. You can apply them if and when you choose. So play around with them. Experiment. Test them out in your life, and see how they work for you. And don't believe they're effective just because I say so; give them a try and trust your own experience.

I should also warn you that as you work through this book, there is one key point I'll be repeating again and again: you won't change your life simply by reading this book. To do that, you will have to take action. It's like reading a travel guide about India: by the end of it, you have a lot of ideas about where you'd like to visit, but you still haven't been there. To truly experience India, you have to make the effort to get up and go there. Similarly, if all you do is read this book and think about the contents, then by the end, you will have a lot of ideas about how to create a rich, full, and meaningful life, but you won't actually be living one. In order to live a better life, you will need to follow through on the exercises and suggestions within these pages. So, are you eager to begin? Then read on . . .

4

The Great Storyteller

This morning I held a fresh lemon in my hands. I ran my fingers over the bright yellow skin, noting all the little dimples. I lifted it to my nose and inhaled the delicious aroma. Then I placed it on a cutting board and sliced it in half. Picking up one of the pieces, I opened my mouth and squeezed a drop of fresh lemon juice onto the tip of my tongue.

• • • • •

What happened as you read about that lemon? Perhaps you "saw" its shape and color. Or maybe you "felt" the texture of the skin. You may have "smelled" the fresh, lemony scent. You may even have found your mouth watering. However, there was no lemon in front of you, only words about a lemon. Yet once those words entered your head, you reacted to them almost as you would to a real lemon.

The same thing happens when you read a great thriller. All you have in front of you are words. But once those words enter your mind, interesting things start to happen. You may "see" or "hear" the characters and experience powerful emotions. When those words describe a character in a dangerous situation, you react as if someone really were in danger: your muscles tense, your heartbeat speeds up, your adrenaline rises. (That's why they're called thrillers!) And yet, all you are dealing with in reality are little black marks on a page. Fascinating things, words! But what exactly are they?

Words and Thoughts

Humans rely heavily on words. Other animals use physical gestures and facial expressions and a variety of sounds to communicate, and so do we, but we are the only animal that uses words. Words are basically a complex system of symbols. (A "symbol" means anything that stands for or refers to something else.) So, for example, the word "dog" in English refers to a certain type of animal. In French, "chien" refers to the same animal, as does "cane" in Italian. Three different symbols, all referring to the same thing.

Anything that we can sense, feel, think about, observe, imagine, or interact with can be symbolized by words: time, space, life, death, heaven, hell, places that never existed, current events, and so on. If you know what a word refers to, then you know its meaning, and you can understand it. But if you don't know what a word refers to, then you don't understand it. For example, "axillary hyperhidrosis" is a medical term that most of us don't understand. It means "sweaty armpits." And now that you know what "axillary hyperhidrosis" refers to, you understand the words.

We use words in two different settings: in public, when we're talking, listening, or writing; and in private, when we're thinking. Words on a page, we call "text"; words spoken out loud, we call "speech"; and words inside our head, we call "thoughts."

It's important not to confuse thoughts with the mental pictures or physical feelings that often accompany them. To clarify the difference, here's a little experiment. Take a few moments to think about what you're going to fix for breakfast tomorrow morning. Then, as you're thinking about it, close your eyes and observe your thoughts as they happen. Notice what form they take. Close your eyes and do this for about half a minute.

• • • • •

Okay, what did you notice? You may have noticed "pictures" in your mind; you "saw" yourself cooking or eating, as on a television screen. We'll call these mental pictures "images." Images are not thoughts, although they often occur together. You may also have noticed feelings or sensations in your body, almost as if you were actually preparing or eating breakfast. These, too, are not thoughts; they are sensations. You also probably noticed some words passing through your head, almost like a talking voice. Those words may have described what you intend to eat: "I'll have toast with peanut butter." These words in our heads are what we call "thoughts." To summarize:

> Thoughts = words inside our heads
> Images = pictures inside our heads
> Sensations = feelings inside our bodies.

It's important to remember this distinction, because we deal with these internal experiences in different ways. We'll be focusing on images and sensations later in the book. For now, we're going to look at thoughts.

Humans rely a lot on their thoughts. Thoughts tell us about our life and how to live it. They tell us how we are and how we should be, what to do and what to avoid. And yet, they are nothing more than words, which is why in ACT we often refer to thoughts as stories. Sometimes they are true stories (called "facts"), and sometimes they are false. But most of our thoughts are neither true nor false. Most of them are either stories about how we see life (called "opinions," "attitudes," "judgments," "ideals," "beliefs," "theories," "morals," etc.) or about what we want to do with it (called "plans," "strategies," "goals," "wishes," "values," etc.). In ACT, our main interest in a thought is not whether it's true or false, but whether it's helpful; that is, if we pay attention to this thought, will it help us create the life we want?

The Story Is Not the Event

Imagine that a police officer catches an armed bank robber in a dramatic shoot-out. The next day we read about it in the newspapers. One particular newspaper may give a totally accurate account of what happened. It may have all the facts correct: the name of the police officer, the location of the bank, maybe even the precise number of shots fired. Another newspaper may give a less accurate account of what happened. It may exaggerate some of the details for the sake of drama or just get the facts wrong. But whether the story is totally accurate or false and misleading, it's still just a story. And when we read that story, we aren't actually present at the event. There is no shooting actually taking place before our eyes; all we have in front of us are words and images. The only people who can truly experience this event are those who are present when it happens: the "eyewitnesses." Only an eyewitness actually hears the sound of the shots or sees the gun firing. No matter how detailed the description, the story is not the event (and vice versa).

Of course, we know that newspaper stories are biased. They don't give us the absolute truth; they give us an angle on what happened, which reflects the editorial viewpoint and attitude of the newspaper. We also know that at any point we wish, we can stop reading. If we're not getting anything useful out of the story, we can put down the newspaper and do something constructive.

Now, this may be obvious when it comes to stories in newspapers, but it's not nearly so obvious when it comes to the stories in our minds. All too often we react to our thoughts as if they are the absolute truth or as if we must give them all our attention. The psychological jargon for this reaction is "fusion."

What Is Fusion?

"Fusion" means a blending or melding together. Think of two sheets of metal that are "fused" together. They are stuck to each other; you can't pull them apart. In ACT, we use the term "fusion" to mean that a thought and the thing it refers to—the story and the event—become stuck together, as one. Thus, we react to words about a lemon as if a lemon is actually present; we react to words in a crime novel as if someone really is about to be murdered; we react to words like "I'm useless" as if we actually are useless; and we react to words like "I'm going to fail" as if failure is a foregone conclusion. In a state of fusion, it seems as if:

- Thoughts are reality—what we're thinking is actually happening, here and now.
- Thoughts are the truth—we completely believe them.

- Thoughts are important—we take them seriously and give them our full attention.
- Thoughts are orders—we automatically obey them.
- Thoughts are wise—we assume they know best, and we follow their advice.
- Thoughts can be threats—some thoughts can be deeply disturbing or frightening, and we feel the need to get rid of them.

Remember Michelle, who is plagued by thoughts such as, "I'm hopeless," "I'm a lousy mother," and "Nobody likes me"? In a state of fusion, those thoughts seemed to be the gospel truth. As a result, she felt terrible. "That's not surprising," you might think. "With thoughts like that, anyone would feel upset." Certainly that's what Michelle believed—at first. But she soon discovered that she could instantly reduce the impact of such unpleasant thoughts by applying the simple technique described below. Read through the instructions first, then give it a try.

"I'M HAVING THE THOUGHT THAT . . ."

To begin this exercise, first bring to mind an upsetting thought that takes the form "I am X." For example, "I'm not good enough" or "I'm incompetent." Preferably pick a thought that often recurs and that usually bothers or upsets you. Now focus on that thought and believe it as much as you can for ten seconds.

• • • • •

Next, take that thought and in front of it, insert this phrase: "I'm having the thought that . . ." Play that thought again, but this time with the phrase attached. Think to yourself, "I'm having the thought that I am X." Notice what happens.

• • • • •

Now do that again, but this time the phrase is slightly longer: "I notice I'm having the thought that . . ." Think to yourself, "I notice I'm having the thought that I am X." Notice what happens.

• • • • •

Did you do it? Remember, you can't learn to ride a bike just by reading about it; you actually have to get on the bike and pedal. And you won't get much out of this book if you just read the exercises. To change the way you handle your painful thoughts, you actually have to practice some new skills. So if you haven't done the exercise, please go back and do it now.

• • • • •

So what happened? You probably found that inserting those phrases instantly gave you some distance from the actual thought; as if you "stepped back" from it. (If you didn't notice any difference, try it again with another thought.)

You can use this technique with any unpleasant thought. For instance, if your mind says, "Life sucks!" then simply acknowledge, "I'm having the thought that life sucks!" If your mind says, "I'll fail!" then simply acknowledge, "I'm having the thought that I'll fail!" Using this phrase means you're less likely to get beaten up or pushed around by your thoughts. Instead, you can step back and see those thoughts for what they are: nothing more than words passing through your head. We call this process "defusion." In a state of *fusion* thoughts seem to be *the absolute truth* and *very important*. But in a state of *defusion*, we recognize that:

- Thoughts are merely sounds, words, stories, or bits of language.
- Thoughts may or may not be true; we don't automatically believe them.
- Thoughts may or may not be important; we pay attention only if they're helpful.
- Thoughts are definitely not orders; we certainly don't have to obey them.
- Thoughts may or may not be wise; we don't automatically follow their advice.
- Thoughts are never threats; even the most painful or disturbing of thoughts does not represent a threat to us.

In ACT we have many different techniques to facilitate defusion. Some of them may seem a bit gimmicky at first, but think of them like training wheels on a bicycle: once you can ride the bike, you don't need them anymore. So try out each technique as we come to it and see which works best for you. Remember as you use the techniques, the aim of defusion is not to get rid of a thought, but simply to see it for what it is—just a string of words—and to let it be there without fighting it.

The next technique calls on your musical abilities. But don't worry, no one will be listening except you.

MUSICAL THOUGHTS

Bring to mind a negative self-judgment that commonly bothers you when it comes up. For example, "I'm such an idiot." Now hold that thought in your mind and really believe it as much as you can for about ten seconds. Notice how it affects you.

• • • • •

Now imagine taking that same thought and singing it to yourself to the tune of "Happy Birthday." Sing it silently inside your head. Notice what happens.

• • • • •

Now go back to the thought in its original form. Once again, hold it in your mind and believe it as much as you can, for about ten seconds. Notice how it affects you.

• • • • •

Now imagine taking that thought and singing it to the tune of "Jingle Bells." Sing it silently inside your head. Notice what happens.

• • • • •

After doing this exercise, you probably found that by now you're just not taking that thought quite so seriously; you're just not buying into it as much. Notice that you haven't challenged the thought at all. You haven't tried to get rid of it, debated whether it's true or false, or tried to replace it with a positive thought. So what has happened? Basically, you have "defused" it. By taking the thought and putting it to music, you have realized that it is just made up of words, like the lyrics of a song.

The Mind Is a Great Storyteller

The mind loves telling stories; in fact, it never stops. All day, every day, it tells you stories about what you should be doing with your life, what other people think of you, what will happen in the future, what went wrong in the past, and so on. It's like a radio that never stops broadcasting.

Unfortunately, a lot of these stories are really negative—stories such as, "I'm not good enough," "I can't do it," "I'm so fat," "My life is terrible," "I will fail," "Nobody likes me," "This relationship is doomed," "I can't cope," "I'll never be happy," etc.

There's nothing abnormal in this. Our minds evolved to think negatively, and research shows that about 80 percent of our thoughts have some degree of negative content. But you can see how these stories, if taken as the absolute truth, can readily feed into anxiety, depression, anger, low self-esteem, self-doubt, and insecurity.

Most psychological approaches regard negative stories as a major problem and make a big fuss about trying to eliminate them. Such approaches will advise you to try to rewrite the story, making it more positive, get rid of the story by repeatedly telling yourself a better one, distract yourself from the story, push the story away, or argue with the story and debate whether it's true or not. But haven't you already tried methods like these? The reality is, they simply will not get rid of negative stories in the long run. In ACT the approach is very different. Negative stories are not seen as a problem in their own right. It's only when we "fuse" with them, when we react as if they were the truth and give them our full attention, that they become problematic.

When we read about celebrities in the tabloids, we know that many of the stories are false or misleading. Some are exaggerated for effect, others are made up entirely. Now some celebrities take this in their stride; they accept it as part of being famous and don't let it get to them. When they notice ridiculous stories about themselves, they just shrug it off. They certainly don't waste their time reading, analyzing, and discussing them! Other celebrities, though, get very upset about these stories. They read them and dwell on them, rant and complain, and lodge lawsuits (which are stressful and eat up a lot of time, energy, and money).

Defusion allows us to be like the first set of celebrities: the stories are there, but we don't take them seriously. We don't pay them much attention, and we certainly don't waste our time and energy trying to fight them. In ACT we don't try to avoid or get rid of the story. We know how ineffective that is. Instead we simply acknowledge: "This is a story."

NAMING YOUR STORIES

Identify your mind's favorite stories, then give them names, such as the "loser!" story, or the "my life sucks!" story, or the "I can't do it!" story. Often there will be several variations on a theme. For example, the "nobody likes me" story may show up as "I'm boring," the "I'm undesirable" story as "I'm fat," and the "I'm inadequate" story as "I'm stupid." When your stories show up, acknowledge them by name. For example, you could say to yourself, "Ah yes. I recognize this. That old favorite, the 'I'm a failure' story." Or "Aha! Here comes the 'I can't cope' story." Once you've acknowledged a story, that's it—just let it be. You don't have to challenge it or push it away, nor do you have to give it much attention. Simply let it come and go as it pleases, while you channel your energy into doing something you value.

Michelle, whom we met earlier, identified two major stories: the "I'm worthless" story, and the "I'm unlovable" story. Acknowledging her thoughts by these names made her far less likely to get caught up in them. But Michelle's hands-down favorite technique was Musical Thoughts. Whenever she caught herself buying into the "I'm so pathetic" story, she would put the words to music and watch them instantly lose all their power. And she didn't just stick to "Happy Birthday." She experimented with a wide variety of tunes, from Beethoven to the Beatles. After a week of practicing this technique repeatedly throughout the day, she found she was taking those thoughts a lot less seriously (even without the music). They hadn't gone away, but they bothered her much less.

Now you're no doubt brimming with all sorts of questions. But be patient. In the next few chapters we're going to cover defusion in much more detail, including how to use it with mental images. In the meantime, practice using the three techniques we've covered so far: I'm Having the Thought That . . . , Musical Thoughts, and Naming the Story.

Of course, if you don't like a particular technique, you can leave it. And if you have a favorite, you can stick to it. Use these techniques regularly with distressing thoughts, at least ten times a day when starting. Anytime you're feeling stressed, anxious, or depressed, ask yourself, "What story is my mind telling me now?" Then once you've identified it, defuse it.

It's important not to build up great expectations at this point. At times defusion occurs easily; at other times it may not happen at all. So play around with these methods and notice what happens—but don't expect instant transformation.

If all this seems too difficult, just acknowledge, "I'm having the thought that it's too difficult!" It's okay to have the thought that "It's too hard," or that "This is stupid," or that "It won't work." They're all just thoughts, so see them for what they are and let them be.

"That's all fine," you may say, "but what if the thoughts are true?"

Good question.

5

True Blues

In ACT, whether a thought is true is not that important. Far more important is whether it's helpful. Truthful or not, thoughts are nothing more than words. If they're helpful words, then it's worth paying attention to them. If they're not helpful, then why bother?

Suppose I am making some serious mistakes in my work and my mind tells me, "You are incompetent!" This is not a helpful thought. It doesn't tell me what I can do to improve the situation; it's merely demoralizing. Putting myself down is pointless. Instead, what I need to do is to take action: brush up on my skills or ask for help.

Or suppose I'm overweight and my mind says, "You're a lump of lard! Just look at that belly—it's disgusting!" This thought is not helpful; it does nothing but blame, disparage, and demoralize. It doesn't inspire me to eat sensibly or exercise more; it just makes me feel lousy.

You can waste a lot of time trying to decide whether your thoughts are actually true; again and again your mind will try to suck you into that debate. But although at times this is important, most of the time it is irrelevant and wastes a lot of energy.

The more useful approach is to ask, "Is this thought helpful? Does it help me take action to create the life I want?" If it's helpful, pay attention. If it's not, defuse it. "But," I hear you ask, "what if that negative thought actually is helpful? What if telling myself, 'I'm fat' actually prompts me to lose some weight?" Fair enough. If a negative thought *does* actually motivate you, then by all means make use of it. But almost always, self-critical thoughts of this nature do not motivate us to take effective action. Usually such thoughts (if we fuse with them) just make us feel guilty, stressed, depressed, frustrated, or anxious. And usually people with weight problems react to those unpleasant emotions by eating *even more* food, in a futile attempt to feel better! In ACT we place great emphasis on taking effective action to improve your quality of life. In later chapters we'll look at how to do this. For now, suffice to say, thoughts that criticize you, insult you, judge you, put you down, or blame you are likely to lower your motivation rather than increase it. So when troublesome thoughts pop into your head, it may be useful to ask yourself one or more of the following questions:

- Is this an old thought? Have I heard this one before? Do I gain anything useful from listening to it again?
- Does this thought help me take effective action to improve my life?
- What would I get for buying into this thought?

At this point you may be wondering, how can you tell whether a thought is helpful or not? If you're not sure, you can ask yourself:

- Does it help me to be the person I want to be?
- Does it help me to build the sort of relationships I'd like?
- Does it help me to connect with what I truly value?
- Does it help me, in the long term, to create a rich, full, and meaningful life?

If the answer to any of these questions is yes, then the thought is probably helpful. (And if not, it's probably *un*helpful.)

Thoughts Are Just Stories

In chapter 4, I discussed the concept that thoughts are basically just "stories"—a bunch of words strung together to tell us something. But if thoughts are just stories, then how do we know which ones to believe? There are three parts to this answer. First, be wary of holding on to any belief too tightly. We all have beliefs, but the more tightly we hold on to them, the more inflexible we become in our attitudes and behaviors. If you've ever tried having an argument with someone who absolutely believes they are right, then you know how pointless it is—they will never see any point of view other than their own. We describe them as being inflexible, rigid, narrow-minded, blinkered, or "stuck in their ways."

Also, if you reflect on your own experience, you'll recognize that your beliefs change over time; that is, the beliefs that you once held tightly, you may now find laughable. For instance, at some point you probably used to believe in Santa Claus, the Easter bunny, the tooth fairy, or dragons, goblins, and vampires. And almost everyone changes some of their beliefs about religion, politics, money, family, or health at some point, as they grow older. So by all means, have your beliefs—but hold them lightly. Keep in mind that all beliefs are stories, whether or not they're "true."

Second, if a thought helps you to create a rich, full, and meaningful life, then use it. Pay attention to it, and use it for guidance and motivation—and at the same time remember that it is still just a story; a bit of human language. So use it, but don't clutch it too tightly.

Third, in ACT we urge you to pay careful attention to what is *actually happening*, rather than just automatically believing what your mind says. For example, you may have heard of the "impostor syndrome." This is where someone who does his job competently and effectively believes that he's just an impostor; that he doesn't really know what he's doing. The impostor thinks of himself as a fraud, bluffing his way through everything, always on the verge of being "found out." People with impostor syndrome are not paying enough attention to their direct experience, to the clearly observable facts that they are doing their job effectively. Instead they are paying attention to an overcritical mind that says, "You don't know what you're doing. Sooner or later everyone will see you're a fake."

In my early years as a doctor, I had a bad case of impostor syndrome. If one of my patients said, "Thank you. You're a wonderful doctor," I used to think, "Yeah, right. You wouldn't say that if you knew what I'm really like." I could never accept such compliments, because although in reality I did my job well, my mind kept telling me I was useless, and I believed it.

Whenever I made a mistake, no matter how trivial, two words would automatically blaze into my head: "I'm incompetent." Back then, I used to get really upset, believing that thought was the absolute truth. Then I'd start doubting myself and stressing out about all the decisions I'd made. Had I misdiagnosed that stomachache? Had I prescribed the wrong antibiotic? Had I overlooked something serious?

Sometimes I would argue with the thought. I'd point out that everyone makes mistakes, including doctors, and that none of the mistakes I made was ever serious, and that overall I did my job very well. At other times I would run through lists of all the things I did well and remind myself of all the positive feedback I'd had from my patients and colleagues. Or I'd repeat positive affirmations about my abilities. But none of that got rid of the negative thought or stopped it from bothering me.

These days the same two words still often pop up when I make a mistake, but the difference is now they don't bother me—because I don't take them seriously. I know that those words are just an automatic response, like the way your eyes shut whenever you sneeze. The fact is, we don't choose most of the thoughts in our head. We do choose a small number of them, when we're actively planning or mentally rehearsing or being creative, but most of the thoughts in our head just "show up" of their own accord. We have many thousands of useless or unhelpful thoughts every day. And no matter how harsh, cruel, silly, vindictive, critical, frightening, or downright weird they may be, we can't prevent them from popping up. But just because they appear doesn't mean we have to take them seriously.

In my case, the "I'm incompetent" story was there long before I became a doctor. In many different aspects of my life, from learning to dance to using a computer, any mistake I've made has triggered the same thought: "I'm incompetent." Of course, it's not always those exact words. Often it's variants on the same theme, such as: "Idiot!" or "Can't you do anything right?" But these thoughts are not a problem as long as I see them for what they really are: just a few words that popped into my head. Basically, the more tuned in you are to your direct experience of life (rather than to your mind's running commentary), the more empowered you are to take your life in the direction you truly want. In later chapters you will learn how to develop this ability.

The Stories Never Stop

The mind never stops telling stories—not even when we're asleep. It is constantly comparing, judging, evaluating, criticizing, planning, pontificating, and fantasizing. And many of the stories it tells are real attention grabbers. Time and time again we get lost in these stories—a process for which we have many different expressions. We speak of being preoccupied or "lost in thought," of "struggling with an idea," "buying into a concept," or getting "carried away" by our thoughts. These expressions illustrate how our thoughts take up so much time, energy, and attention. Most of the time we take our thoughts far too seriously and give them far too much attention. The following exercise demonstrates the difference between attaching importance to a thought and not taking a thought seriously.

NOT TAKING A THOUGHT SERIOUSLY

Bring to mind a thought that normally upsets you, that takes the form "I am X" (for example, "I am inadequate"). Hold that thought in your mind and notice how it affects you.

• • • • •

Now bring to mind the thought, "I am a banana!" Hold it in your mind and notice how it affects you.

• • • • •

What did you notice? Most people find that the first thought bothers them but the second thought makes them grin. Why? Because you don't take the second thought seriously. But if the words following "I am" are "a loser," "a failure," "a fat pig," or "a boring person," instead of "a banana," we attach far more importance to them. And yet, they are all just words. The following two techniques provide simple ways of taking your thoughts less seriously.

THANKING YOUR MIND

This is a simple and effective defusion technique. When your mind starts coming up with those same old stories, simply thank it. You could say to yourself (silently) things such as, "Thank you, Mind! How very informative!" or "Thanks for sharing!" or "Is that right? How fascinating!" or simply, "Thanks, Mind!"

When thanking your mind, don't do it sarcastically or aggressively. Do it with warmth and humor and with a genuine appreciation for the amazing storytelling ability of your mind. (You could also combine this technique with Naming the Story: "Ah yes, the 'I'm a failure' story. Thanks so much, Mind!")

Below is another technique that will help you take your thoughts less seriously. Read through the instructions first and then give it a go.

THE SILLY VOICES TECHNIQUE

This technique is particularly good with recurrent negative self-judgments. Find a thought that upsets or bothers you. Focus on the thought for ten seconds, believing it as much as possible. Notice how it affects you.

• • • • •

Then pick an animated cartoon character with a humorous voice, such as Mickey Mouse, Bugs Bunny, Shrek, or Homer Simpson. Now bring the troubling thought to mind, but "hear" it in the cartoon character's voice, as if that character were speaking your thoughts out loud. Notice what happens.

• • • • •

Now get the negative thought back in its original form and again believe it as much as possible. Notice how it affects you.

• • • • •

Next pick a different cartoon character or a character from a movie or television show. Consider fantasy characters such as Darth Vader, Yoda, Gollum, or someone from your favorite sitcom, or actors with distinctive voices, such as Arnold Schwarzenegger or Eddie Murphy. Once again bring the distressing thought to mind and "hear" it in that voice. Notice what happens.

• • • • •

After doing this exercise and then repeating it, you've probably found that you're not taking that negative thought quite so seriously. You may even have found yourself grinning or chuckling. Notice that you haven't tried to change the thought, get rid of it, argue with it, push it away, debate whether it's true or false, replace it with a more positive thought, or distract yourself from it in any way. You have merely seen it for what it is: a bit of language. By taking that segment of language and hearing it in a different voice, you become aware that it is nothing more than a string of words—and thus, it loses its impact. (This may remind you of a rhyme we learned as children: "Sticks and stones may break my bones, but words can never hurt me." Unfortunately, as children we couldn't put this into practice all that well, because no one ever taught us defusion skills.)

A client of mine—we'll call her Jana—who suffered from depression, found this method extremely helpful. She had grown up with a verbally abusive mother who constantly criticized and insulted her. The insults that had once come from her mother had now turned into recurrent negative thoughts: "You're fat," "You're ugly," "You're stupid," "You'll never amount to anything," "Nobody likes you." When these thoughts came to mind during our sessions, Jana would often start crying. She had spent many years (and thousands of dollars) in therapy, trying to get rid of these thoughts, all to no avail.

Jana was an avid fan of the comedy troupe Monty Python, and the character she picked was from their film *The Life of Brian*. In the film, Brian's mother, played by the male actor Terry Jones, is always criticizing Brian in a ridiculously high-pitched, screeching voice. When Jana "heard" her negative thoughts in the voice of Brian's mother, she couldn't take them seriously. The thoughts did not immediately disappear, but they quickly lost their power over her, and this contributed significantly to lifting her depression.

But what if a thought is both true and serious? For instance, if you are dying from cancer and have the thought: "I'll be dead soon." From an ACT perspective, we are far more interested in whether a thought is helpful than whether it's true or false, serious or ridiculous, negative or positive, optimistic or pessimistic. The bottom line is always the same: does this thought help you make the most out of life? Now, if you only have a few months to live, it's really important to reflect on how you want to spend them. What loose ends do you need to tie up? What do you want to do, and whom do you want to see before you die? So a thought like, "I'll be dead soon" could be helpful if it motivates you to reflect and take effective action. If that's the case, you wouldn't try to defuse such a thought. You would pay attention to it and use it to help you do what you need to do. But suppose that thought becomes an obsession, and you keep playing it over and over in your head. Would it be helpful to spend your last weeks of life thinking all day long, "I'll be dead soon," giving all your attention to that thought instead of to the loved ones around you?

Now, for some people the Silly Voices technique may seem inappropriate for a thought like this, because it might seem to be trivializing something quite serious. If that's how it feels to you, don't use it. But it's important to note that defusion is not about trivializing or making fun of genuine problems in your life. Defusion is aimed at freeing ourselves from the oppression of our thoughts; freeing up our time, energy, and attention so we can invest them in meaningful activities rather than dwelling uselessly on our thoughts. So if the thought, "I'll be dead soon" keeps showing up and taking up all your attention, thus preventing you from connecting with your loved ones, then you could defuse it in a number of different ways. You could acknowledge, "Aha! Here's the 'imminent death' story" or "I'm having the thought that I'll be dead soon" or you could simply say, "Thanks, Mind!"

And don't think you are going to have to spend the rest of your life thanking your mind or hearing your thoughts in ditties and silly voices.

These methods are merely stepping-stones. Down the line you can expect to defuse your thoughts instantly, without the need for such contrived techniques (although there will always be times when it's useful to pull them out of your psychological tool kit).

When practicing defusion, it's important to keep the following things in mind:

- The aim of defusion is not to get rid of unpleasant thoughts, but rather to see them for what they are—just words—and to let go of struggling with them. At times they will go away quickly, and at times they won't. If you start expecting them to go, you are setting yourself up for disappointment or frustration.
- Don't expect these techniques to make you feel good. Often when you defuse a troublesome thought, you will feel better. But this is just a beneficial by-product, not the main goal. The main goal of defusion is to disentangle you from unhelpful thought processes, so you can focus your attention on more important things. So when defusion does make you feel better, by all means enjoy it. But don't expect it to. And don't start using it to try to control how you feel; otherwise, you're stuck right back in the happiness trap.
- Remember that you're human, so there will be plenty of times when you forget to use these new skills. And that's okay, because the moment you realize you've been reeled in by unhelpful thoughts, you can instantly use one of these techniques to unhook yourself.
- Remember that no technique is foolproof. There may be times when you try them and defusion doesn't happen. If so, simply observe what it's like to be fused with your thoughts. Merely learning to tell the difference between fusion and defusion is useful in its own right.

Defusion is like any other skill: the more you practice, the better you get. So add the Thanking Your Mind and Silly Voices techniques to your repertoire and aim to use them between five and ten times each day.

At this point, don't expect any dramatic changes in your life. Simply notice what happens as you incorporate these practices into your daily routine. And if you're having any doubts or concerns, make a note of them. In the next chapter we'll look at common problems people have with defusion and, more importantly, we'll learn how to overcome them.

6

Troubleshooting Defusion

"Defusion doesn't work!" snapped John.

"What do you mean?" I asked.

"Well," he said, "I had to give this presentation at work in front of about fifty people. My mind kept telling me I was going to screw up and make a fool of myself, so I tried those defusion techniques, but they did nothing."

"You mean, you kept buying into the story that you'd screw up?"

"No, it helped with that—I stopped taking it seriously."

"Then why do you say defusion doesn't work?"

"Because I still felt anxious."

"John," I said, "I've been giving talks in public for over twenty years, and I still feel anxious every time I get up there. I've met hundreds of people who speak to audiences as part of their profession, and I've always asked them, "Do you get anxious when you give a talk?" So far, almost every single person has said yes. The point is, if you're going to put yourself in any sort of challenging situation, if you're going to take any significant risk, then anxiety is a normal emotion. It will be there. And defusing negative thoughts is not going to get rid of it."

Many of us, when we first encounter defusion, fall into the same trap as John; we start trying to use defusion as a control strategy, as a way of trying to make our experience different than it is. Remember: A control strategy is any attempt to change, avoid, or get rid of unwanted thoughts and feelings.

Control strategies become problematic when they are used excessively or inappropriately or in situations where they can't work, or when using them reduces our quality of life in the long term. Defusion is the very opposite of a control strategy; it's an acceptance strategy. In ACT, rather than attempting to change, avoid, or get rid of unpleasant thoughts and feelings, our aim is to accept them. Acceptance doesn't mean you have to like your uncomfortable thoughts and feelings; it just means you stop struggling with them. When you stop wasting your energy on trying to change, avoid, or get rid of them, you can put that energy into something more useful instead. This is best explained with an analogy.

Imagine you live in a small country that shares a border with a hostile neighbor. There is long-standing tension between the two countries. The neighboring country has a different religion and a different political system, and your country sees it as a major threat. There are three possible scenarios for how your country can relate to its neighbor.

The worst-case scenario is war. Your country attacks, and the other one retaliates (or vice versa). As both countries get pulled into a major war, the people of both nations suffer. Think of any major war and the huge costs involved in terms of life, money, and well-being.

Another scenario, better than the first but still far from satisfactory, is a temporary truce. Both countries agree to a cease-fire, but there is no reconciliation. Resentment seethes beneath the surface, and there is the constant underlying threat that war will break out again. Think of India and Pakistan with the constant threat of nuclear war and the intense hostility between Hindus and Muslims.

The third possibility is genuine peace. You acknowledge your differences and allow them just to be. This doesn't get rid of the other country, nor does it mean that you necessarily like it or even want it there. Nor does it mean that you approve of its politics or religion. But because you're no longer at war, you can now use your money and resources to build up the infrastructure of your own country, instead of squandering them on the battlefield.

The first scenario, war, is like the struggle to get rid of unwanted thoughts and feelings. It's a battle that can never be won, and it consumes a huge amount of time and energy.

The second scenario, a truce, is definitely better, but it's still a long way from true acceptance. It's more like a grudging tolerance; there's no sense of moving forward to a new future. Although there is no active warfare, the hostility remains, and you are resigned to the ongoing tension. A grudging tolerance of thoughts and feelings is better than an outright struggle, but it leaves you feeling stuck and somewhat helpless. It's a sense more of resignation than of acceptance, of entrapment rather than freedom, of being stuck rather than moving forward.

The third scenario, peace, represents true acceptance. Notice that in this scenario your country doesn't have to like the other country, approve of its being there, convert to its religion, or learn to speak its language. You simply make peace with them. You acknowledge your differences, you give up trying to change their politics or religion, and you focus your efforts on making your own country a better place to live in. It's the same when you truly accept your uncomfortable thoughts and feelings. You don't have to like them, want them, or approve of them; you simply make peace with them and let them be. This leaves you free to focus your energy on taking action—action that moves your life forward in a direction you value.

The True Meaning of Acceptance

Acceptance does not mean putting up with or resigning yourself to anything. Acceptance is about embracing life, not merely tolerating it. Acceptance literally means "taking what is offered." It doesn't mean giving up or admitting defeat; it doesn't mean just gritting your teeth and bearing it. It means fully opening yourself to your present reality—acknowledging how it is, right here and now, and letting go of the struggle with life as it is in this moment.

But what if you want to improve your life and not just accept it as it is? Well, that's the whole purpose of this book. But the most effective way to make changes in your life is to start by fully accepting it. Suppose you are walking across ice. In order to safely take the next step, you first need to find a firm foothold. If you try moving forward without doing that, then you're likely to fall flat on your face.

Acceptance is like finding that firm foothold. It's a realistic appraisal of where your feet are and what condition the ground is in. It doesn't mean that you like being in that spot, or that you intend to stay there. Once you have a firm foothold, you can take the next step more effectively. The more fully you accept the reality of your situation—as it is, here and now—the more effectively you can take action to change it.

The Dalai Lama exemplifies this beautifully. He fully accepts that China has invaded Tibet and that he is forced to live in exile from his own country. He doesn't waste time and energy in wishful thinking, getting outraged, or dwelling morosely on what he's lost. He knows that won't help. Nor does he admit defeat or throw the whole issue into the "too-hard basket." Instead he acknowledges that right now this is the way it is, and at the same time he does everything in his power to improve the situation. He actively campaigns all around the world to increase public and political awareness of Tibet's predicament and to raise financial support for its people.

In another example, let's consider the case of domestic violence. If your partner is physically violent, the first step is to accept the reality of the situation: that you are in danger and you need to take action to protect yourself. The next step is to take action: get some professional help, take legal action, and/or leave the relationship. In order to take this action, you will need to accept the anxiety, guilt, and other painful thoughts and feelings that are likely to rise. So this is what ACT is all about: acceptance and action, side by side. The core philosophy of ACT is neatly encapsulated in the Serenity Challenge (my version of the well-known Serenity Prayer):

> Develop the courage to solve those problems that can be solved, the serenity to accept those problems that can't be solved, and the wisdom to know the difference.

If your life isn't working for you, the only sensible thing is to take action to change it. That action will be far more effective when you start from a place of acceptance. All the time and energy that you waste on struggling with thoughts and feelings could be far more usefully invested in taking effective action.

How to Use Defusion

Now let's return to John's comment that "defusion doesn't work." John was trying to use defusion to get rid of his anxiety. No wonder it "didn't work"! Defusion is not some clever way to control your feelings. It's simply an acceptance technique. True, defusing unhelpful thoughts will often reduce feelings of anxiety, but that's just a beneficial by-product. If you try to use defusion to control your feelings, sooner or later you'll end up frustrated.

So what if you've defused a thought and it doesn't leave? Again, defusion isn't about getting rid of thoughts. It's about seeing them for what they really are and making peace with them; allowing them to be there without fighting them. Sometimes they will go away with very little fuss, other times they will hang around for quite a while. And sometimes they'll go away and then come back again. The point is, once you allow them to be there without a struggle, you can put your energy and attention into activities you value. But if you expect that defusing your thoughts will make them go away, you're setting yourself up for disappointment; you're falling back into the happiness trap.

Remember, you don't have to like a thought in order to accept it. It's okay to want to get rid of it. In fact, it's expected. But wanting to get rid of something is quite different from actively struggling with it. For example, suppose you have an old car that you no longer want. And suppose you won't have an opportunity to sell it for at least another month. You can want to get rid of the car and simultaneously accept that you still have the car. You don't have to try to smash the car up, make yourself miserable, or get drunk every night just because you still have that old car.

So if you do find yourself struggling with a negative thought, just notice it. Pretend that you're a curious scientist observing your own mind; notice the different ways in which you struggle. Do you judge your thoughts as good or bad, true or false, positive or negative? Do you try to push them away or replace them with "better" ones? Do you enter into a debate with them? Observe your struggle with interest and notice what it accomplishes.

Of course, some stories are more persistent than others. I've had my "I'm incompetent" story since I was a child. It visits me much less often these days, but it still pops in from time to time. However, now it doesn't bother me because I don't fuse with it.

It's important to let go of any expectation that your stories will go away or show up less frequently. As it happens, very often they will go away. But if you're defusing them to make them go away, then by definition you're not truly accepting them. And you know where that leads.

"But," I hear you ask, "aren't positive thoughts better than negative thoughts?" Not necessarily. Remember, the most important question is: "Is this thought helpful?" Suppose an alcoholic brain surgeon thinks to himself, "Hey, I'm the greatest brain surgeon in the world. I can do brilliant surgery even if I've been drinking." It's a positive thought, but surely not a helpful one. Most people convicted of drunk driving have had positive thoughts of a similar nature.

The same applies to neutral thoughts. In this book I mostly talk about negative thoughts, simply because they're the ones we most often have problems with. But anything that applies to negative thoughts also applies to neutral and positive thoughts. The bottom line is not whether a thought is positive or negative, true or false, pleasant or unpleasant, optimistic or pessimistic, but whether it helps you create a fulfilling life.

So should you believe any of your thoughts? Yes, but only if they're helpful—and hold those beliefs lightly. And even while you're holding them, know that they are nothing more than language.

As time goes on and you work through the rest of this book, you will learn to defuse unhelpful thoughts quickly and easily. But it's important to remember: fusion is not the enemy. When you're absorbed in making plans or solving problems, or you're lost in a book or a movie, or you're engrossed in a great conversation, or you're pleasantly daydreaming in a hammock—all these life-enhancing activities involve fusion. So fusion is not the enemy; it's only a problem when it stops you living your life fully.

Negative thoughts are not the enemy, either. Because of the way our minds have evolved, many of our thoughts are negative to some extent, so if you consider them to be the enemy, you're always going to be battling with yourself. Thoughts are merely words, symbols, or bits of language, so why declare war on them? Our aim here is to increase our self-awareness, to recognize when we're fusing with our thoughts and to catch ourselves when it happens. Once we have that awareness, we then have a much greater choice as to how we act. If thoughts are helpful, make use of them; if they are unhelpful, then defuse them.

Keep in mind that the defusion techniques we've covered so far are like those inflatable armbands young children use in swimming pools: once you can swim, you don't need them anymore. The idea is that later on, as you incorporate the other ideas within this book, you can defuse your thoughts without giving them too much attention. You can be thoroughly engaged in your work, a conversation, or any other meaningful activity, and when an unhelpful thought pops into your head, you can instantly see it for what it is and let it come and go without it distracting you.

This will be much clearer in the next chapter in which we explore an immensely powerful aspect of human consciousness, a resource within us that has been so overlooked by Western society that there isn't even a common word for it in the English language.

But don't turn the page right away. Why not wait a few days before reading on and in the meantime practice your defusion skills? And if your mind says, "It's all too hard; I can't be bothered," simply thank it.

7

Look Who's Talking

Did anyone ever chide you for not listening? And did you ever reply, "Sorry, I was somewhere else"? Well, if you were "somewhere else," then where were you? And how did you get back again?

ACT answers these questions by teaching you to recognize two different parts of yourself: the "thinking self" and the "observing self." The thinking self is the part of you that thinks, plans, judges, compares, creates, imagines, visualizes, analyzes, remembers, daydreams, and fantasizes. A more common name for it is the "mind." Popular psychological approaches such as positive thinking, cognitive therapy, creative visualization, hypnosis, and neuro-linguistic programming all focus on controlling the way your thinking self operates. This is all great in theory and it appeals to our common sense, but as we have seen, the thinking self is just not that easy to control. (Again, it's not that we have no control—after all, throughout this book we look at many ways to think more effectively—it's just that we have much less control than the "experts" would have us believe.)

The observing self is fundamentally different from the thinking self. The observing self is aware, but does not think; it is the part of you that is responsible for focus, attention, and awareness. While it can observe or pay attention to your thoughts, it can't produce them. Whereas the thinking self thinks about your experience, the observing self registers your experience directly.

For example, if you are playing tennis and you are truly focused, then all your attention is riveted on that ball coming toward you. This is your observing self at work. You are not thinking about the ball; you are observing it.

Now, suppose thoughts start popping into your head like, "I hope my grip is correct," "I'd better make this a good hit," or "Wow, that ball is moving fast!" That is your thinking self at work. And of course, such thoughts can often be distracting. If your observing self pays too much attention to those thoughts, then it is no longer focused on the ball, and your performance will be impaired. (How often have you been focused on a task, only to be distracted by a thought such as, "I hope I don't screw this up!"?)

Or suppose you're watching a magnificent sunset. There are moments when your mind is quiet; when you're simply noticing the spectacle before you. This is your observing self at work: observing, not thinking. But those silent moments don't last long. Your thinking self kicks in: "Wow, look at all those colors! This reminds me of that sunset we saw on vacation last year. I wish I had my camera." And the more attention your observing self pays to the running commentary of the thinking self, the more you lose direct contact with that sunset.

Although we all understand words such as "awareness," "focus," and "attention," most of us in the Western world have little or no concept of the observing self. As a result, there is no common word for it in the English language. We only have the word "mind," which is generally used to denote both the thinking self and the observing self, without distinguishing between the two. To reduce confusion, whenever I use the word "mind" in this book, I am referring only to the thinking self. When I use terms like "attention," "awareness," "observing," "noticing," and "direct experience," I'm referring to various aspects of the observing self. As this book progresses, you will learn how to tune in and use this amazingly potent part of you. Let's begin right now with a simple exercise.

THINKING VERSUS OBSERVING

Close your eyes for about a minute and simply notice what your mind does. Stay on the lookout for any thoughts or images, as if you were a wildlife photographer waiting for an exotic animal to emerge from the undergrowth. If no thoughts or images appear, keep watching; sooner or later they will show themselves—I guarantee it. Notice where those thoughts or images seem to be located: in front of you, above you, behind you, to one side of you, or within you. Once you've done this for a minute, open your eyes again.

That's all there is to it. So read through these instructions once again; then put down the book and give it a try.

● ● ● ● ●

What you experienced were two distinct processes going on. First there was the process of thinking—in other words, some thoughts or images appeared. Then there was the process of observing; that is, you were able to notice or observe those thoughts and images. It's important to experience the distinction between thinking and observing, because as the book goes on, we'll be using each process in different ways. So try the above exercise once more. Close your eyes for about a minute, notice what thoughts or images appear, and notice where they seem to be located.

Hopefully, this little exercise gave you a sense of distance between you and your thoughts: thoughts and images appeared, then disappeared again, and you were able to notice them come and go. Another way of putting this is that your thinking self produced some thoughts, and your observing self observed them.

Our thinking self is a bit like a radio, constantly playing in the background. Most of the time it's the Radio Doom and Gloom Show, broadcasting negative stories twenty-four hours a day. It reminds us of bad things from the past, it warns us of bad things to come in the future, and it gives us regular updates on everything that's wrong with us. Once in a while it broadcasts something useful or cheerful, but not too often. So if we're constantly tuned in to this radio, listening to it intently and, worse, believing everything we hear, then we have a surefire recipe for stress and misery.

Unfortunately, there's no way to switch off this radio. Even Zen masters are unable to achieve such a feat. Sometimes the radio will stop of its own accord for a few seconds (or even—very rarely—for a few minutes). But we just don't have the power to make it stop (unless we short-circuit it with drugs, alcohol, or brain surgery). In fact, generally speaking, the more we try to make this radio stop, the louder it plays.

But there is an alternative approach. Have you ever had a radio playing in the background, but you were so intent on what you were doing that you didn't really listen to it? You could hear the radio playing, but you weren't paying attention to it. In practicing defusion skills, we are ultimately aiming to do precisely that with our thoughts. Once we know that thoughts are just bits of language, we can treat them like background noise—we can let them come and go without focusing on them and without being bothered by them. This is best exemplified by the Thanking Your Mind technique (see chapter 5, page 51): an unpleasant thought appears, but instead of focusing on it, you simply acknowledge its presence, thank your mind, and return your attention to what you're doing.

So here's what we're aiming for with all these defusion skills:

- If the thinking self is broadcasting something unhelpful, the observing self need not pay it much attention. The observing self can simply acknowledge the thought, then turn its attention to what you are doing here and now.
- If the thinking self is broadcasting something useful or helpful, then the observing self can tune in and pay attention.

This is very different from approaches such as positive thinking, which are like airing a second radio show, Radio Happy and Cheerful, alongside Radio Doom and Gloom, in the hope of drowning it out. It's pretty hard to stay focused on what you're doing when you have two radios playing different tunes in the background.

Notice, too, that letting the radio play on without giving it much attention is very different from actively trying to ignore it. Have you ever heard a radio playing and tried not to listen to it? What happened? The more you tried not to hear it, the more it bothered you, right?

The ability to let thoughts come and go in the background while you keep your attention on what you are doing is very useful. Suppose you're in a social situation and your mind is saying, "I'm so boring! I have nothing to say. I wish I could go home!" It's hard to have a good conversation if you're giving all your attention to those thoughts. Similarly, suppose you're learning to drive and your thinking self is saying, "I can't do it. It's too hard. I'm going to crash!" It's hard to drive well if your observing self is focused on those thoughts rather than on the road. The following technique will teach you how to let your thoughts "pass on by" while you keep your attention on what you're doing. First read the instructions, then give it a try.

TEN DEEP BREATHS

Take ten deep breaths, as slowly as possible. (You may prefer to do this with your eyes closed.) Now focus on the rise and fall of your rib cage and the air moving in and out of your lungs. Notice the sensations as the air flows in: your chest rising, your shoulders lifting, your lungs expanding. Notice what you feel as the air flows out: your chest falling, your shoulders dropping, the breath leaving your nostrils. Focus on completely emptying your lungs. Push out every last bit of air, feeling your lungs deflate, and pause for a moment before breathing in again. As you breathe in, notice how your tummy gently pushes outward.

Now let any thoughts and images come and go in the background, as if they were cars passing by outside your house. When a new thought or image appears, briefly acknowledge its presence, as if you were nodding at a passing motorist. As you do this, keep your attention on the breath, following the air, as it flows in and out of your lungs. You may find it helpful to silently say to yourself, "Thinking," whenever a thought or image appears. Many people find this helps them to acknowledge and let go of the thought. Give it a try, and if it's helpful, keep doing it.

From time to time a thought will capture your attention; it will "hook you" and "carry you away" so that you lose track of the exercise. The moment you realize you've been hooked, take a second to notice what distracted you; then gently "unhook" yourself and refocus on your breathing.

Now read through the instructions once more, then put the book down and try this.

• • • • •

How did it go? Most people get hooked up and carried away by their thoughts several times during that exercise. This is how thoughts typically affect us: they reel us in, pulling our attention away from what we're doing. (So although we may say that our mind wanders, this is not accurate. In reality, it's our attention that wanders.)

By regularly practicing this technique, you will learn three important skills: (1) how to let thoughts come and go, without focusing on them, (2) how to recognize when you've been "hooked" by your thoughts, and (3) how to gently "unhook yourself" and refocus your attention.

When practicing this technique, notice the distinction between your thinking self and your observing self. (The observing self focuses on the breath, while the thinking self chatters away in the background.) Notice also that this is an acceptance strategy, not a control strategy. We aren't trying to avoid or get rid of unwanted thoughts; we're simply allowing them to be there, to come and go as they please.

Fortunately, this is an easy technique to practice, because you can do it anytime, anywhere. Therefore aim to practice this exercise throughout the day while you're stuck at traffic lights, waiting in line, on hold on the telephone, waiting for an appointment, during commercial breaks on the TV, and even in bed, last thing at night. Basically, try it anytime you have a moment to spare. (If you don't have time for the full ten breaths, even three or four can be useful.) In particular, try it anytime you realize that you're all caught up in your thoughts. When you're doing this technique, it doesn't matter how many times you get hooked. Each time you notice it and unhook yourself, you're getting more proficient at a valuable skill.

When doing this technique, let go of any expectations; simply notice what effect it has when you do it. Many people find it quite relaxing, but please don't regard it as a relaxation technique. When relaxation occurs, remember, it's merely a beneficial by-product, not the main aim. (Obviously, enjoy it when it does occur, but don't come to expect it, or sooner or later you're bound to be disappointed.)

I've designed the above brief exercises for busy people who say they "don't have enough time in the day" to do formal defusion practice.

However, "not enough time" is just another story. So here's a challenge for you: if you really want to get good at this, then as well as doing all those brief exercises, put aside five minutes twice a day to practice focusing on your breath. For example, you may do five minutes first thing in the morning and five minutes during your lunch break. During these times, keep your attention totally on your breath, while letting your thoughts come and go like passing cars. And each time you notice your attention has wandered, gently refocus. Also, if you haven't already tried it, then try silently saying to yourself, "Thinking," whenever a thought appears. (Some people find this very helpful, but if you don't, then don't bother.)

Realistic Expectations

Your mind will never stop telling you unpleasant stories (at least, not for long)—that's just what minds do. So let's be realistic. The fact is, you will get hooked up and reeled in by these stories again and again.

That's the bad news.

The good news is, you can make dramatic improvements. You can learn to get hooked much less often. You can learn to recognize much faster when you have been hooked, and you can learn to get much better at unhooking yourself! All these abilities will help to keep you out of the happiness trap.

As for the observing self, we've only just begun to scratch the surface. The observing self is a very powerful ally in transforming your life, and we'll return to it many times in later chapters. Meanwhile, we now come to the final chapter on defusion, in which we learn how to deal with . . . scary pictures!

8

Scary Pictures

Roxy trembled. Her face was pale and drawn, her eyes teary.

"What's the diagnosis?" I asked her.

"Multiple sclerosis," she whispered.

Roxy was a thirty-two-year-old lawyer, dedicated to her profession. One day at work she noticed a weakness and numbness in her left leg, and within a few days she was diagnosed with multiple sclerosis or MS. MS is a disease in which the nerves in the body degenerate, creating all sorts of physical problems. In the best-case scenario, you may have one fleeting episode of neurological disturbance from which you fully recover, never to be bothered again. In the worst case, the MS steadily worsens and your nervous system progressively deteriorates, until you are severely physically disabled. Doctors have no way of predicting how it will affect a patient.

Not surprisingly, Roxy was very frightened by this diagnosis. She kept imagining herself in a wheelchair, her body horribly deformed, her mouth twisted and drooling. Every time this image popped into her head, it terrified her. She tried telling herself all the usual commonsense things: "Don't worry, it will probably never happen to you," "Your chances are excellent, cross that bridge if and when you come to it," "What's the point of worrying about something that may never happen?" Friends, family, and doctors also tried to reassure her with similar advice. But did that get rid of this scary image? Not in the least.

Roxy found she could sometimes push the image out of her head, but it wouldn't stay away for long, and when it returned, it seemed to bother her even more than before. This commonly used, but ineffective, control strategy is known as "thought suppression." Thought suppression means actively pushing distressing thoughts or images out of your head. For example, each time an unwanted thought or image appears, you might say to yourself, "No, don't think about it!" or "Stop it!" or you might just mentally shove it away. Research shows that although this method often gets rid of distressing thoughts or images in the short term, after a while there is a rebound effect: the negative thoughts return in greater numbers and intensity than before.

Most of us have a tendency to conjure up frightening images of the future. How often have you "seen yourself" failing, being rejected, getting sick, or getting into trouble of some kind? Unpleasant or unnerving images will pop up again and again whenever we are faced with challenges in life, and we can waste a lot of precious time dwelling on them or trying to get rid of them. Moreover, if we completely fuse with these images, they may seem so frightening that they scare us away from doing the things we value. For example, many people avoid air travel because their minds conjure up images of the plane crashing. In a state of fusion, we:

- Take these images seriously
- Give them all our attention
- React to them as if the events in the picture are actually happening right now

In a state of defusion we:

- Recognize that images are nothing more than pictures.
- Recognize that those pictures cannot harm us in any way.
- Pay attention to them only if they are helpful.

The defusion techniques we use with images are very similar to the ones we use with thoughts. Initially, we need to focus on these images in order to practice defusing them. But the ultimate aim is to be able to let these images come and go without giving them much attention—like having the television on in the background, without really watching it.

Defusion techniques help us to see these images for what they are: nothing more than colorful pictures. Once we recognize this, we can let them be there without fighting them, without judging them, and without trying to avoid them. In other words, we can accept them. Acceptance means we no longer have to fear them, or waste our precious energy on struggling with them.

Before trying out the following techniques, it's important to say a few words about painful memories. We store memories with all five senses: sight, sound, smell, taste, and touch. The techniques that follow are often helpful with visual memories, that is, memories which have been stored primarily as images. However when working with memories, you need to be careful. While the techniques in this chapter are helpful for coming to terms with many unpleasant memories, such as times you have failed, screwed up, been rejected, humiliated, or embarrassed, they may not be appropriate for more traumatic memories. If you are deeply distressed by traumatic memories of rape, torture, child abuse, domestic violence, or other serious incidents, I don't recommend you use these methods by yourself. Instead, you should learn how to defuse such memories with an appropriately trained therapist.

Defusing Unpleasant Images

No technique known to humanity is 100 percent reliable, and defusion techniques are no exception. If you find that a particular technique doesn't work, just notice what it's like to be fused and move on to a different one. For each technique first read through the instructions, then bring to mind a troublesome image that tends to recur. If it's a moving image, condense it into a ten-second "video clip." After reading the instructions for each exercise, put the book down and try the technique. If any technique seems inappropriate, don't do it.

TELEVISION SCREEN

Bring an unpleasant image to mind and notice how it's affecting you. Now imagine there's a small television screen across the room from you. Place your image on the television screen. Play around with the image: flip it upside down, turn it on its side, spin it around and around, stre-e-e-etch it sideways. If it's a moving "video clip," play it in slow motion. Then play it backward in slow motion. Then play it forward at double speed. Then reverse it at double speed. Turn the color down, so it's all in black-and-white. Turn the color and brightness up until it's ridiculously lurid (so the people have bright orange skin and the clouds are hot pink). The idea is not to get rid of this image but to see it for what it is: a harmless picture. You may need to do this for anything from ten seconds to two minutes, until you really defuse it. If at the end of two minutes it's still bothering you, then try the next technique.

SUBTITLES

Keeping that image on the television screen, add a subtitle. For example, an image of you failing might be subtitled: "The Failure Story." Better still, make it a humorous subtitle, like "D'oh! Done it again!" If it's still bothering you at the end of another thirty seconds, try the next technique.

MUSICAL SOUNDTRACK

Keeping that image on the television screen, add a musical soundtrack of your choice. Experiment with a few different soundtracks: jazz, hip-hop, classical, rock, or your favorite movie themes. If the image is still bothering you, try the next technique.

SHIFTING LOCATIONS

Visualize this image in a variety of different locations, staying with each scenario for twenty seconds before shifting to a new one. For example, visualize your image on the T-shirt of a jogger or a rock star. Visualize it painted on a banner, flying behind an airplane. Visualize it as a bumper sticker, as a magazine photo, or as a tattoo on someone's back. Visualize it as a "pop-up" on a computer screen or as a poster in a teenager's bedroom. Visualize it as the image on a postage stamp or as a drawing in a comic book. Use your imagination with this; the sky's the limit.

If you're still fused with the image after all this—that is, if it's still upsetting you, frightening you, or taking up all your attention whenever it appears—then I would suggest you practice running through some or all of the above exercises every single day for at least five minutes. This is what I asked Roxy to do and within a week that image of herself in a wheelchair was no longer bothering her. It still appeared from time to time, but it no longer frightened her, and she was able to let it come and go while she focused on more important things. Paradoxically, the less she tried to push this image away, the less often it appeared. This was not the intention, but it's something that often happens as a positive side effect.

For less troublesome images, you can easily adapt other defusion techniques. Instead of "I'm having the thought that . . ." you can acknowledge, "I'm having the image of . . ." For example, "I'm having the image of screwing up the interview." If the image is a memory, you could try, "I'm having the memory of . . ." You could even try, "My mind's showing me a picture of . . ."

Instead of Naming the Story, you can Name the Picture or Name the Memory. And you can always say, "Thanks, Mind!" for whatever it shows you.

At this point, let's take a moment to recall that defusion is all about acceptance. The idea is not to get rid of these images but to let go of struggling with them. Why should you accept them? Because the reality is, for the rest of your life, in one form or another, scary pictures will appear. Remember, your mind evolved from a "don't get killed" device. It saved your ancestors' hides by sending them warnings: an image of a bear sleeping in the back of that cave or of a hungry sabre-toothed tiger crouched on that rock. So after a hundred thousand years of evolution, your mind is not suddenly going to say, "Oh, hang on a minute. I no longer live in a cave, vulnerable to bears and tigers—I don't need to keep sending out these warnings anymore." Sorry, but minds don't work like that.

Again, don't believe this just because I say so. Check your own experience. Despite everything you've tried over the years, isn't it a fact that your mind still produces unpleasant pictures? So we need to learn how to live with these things—to pay them attention if they're helpful, or let them come and go if they're not.

And once again, I have to prepare you. When you practice these techniques, your unpleasant images will often disappear, or at least reduce in frequency, and you will often feel much better. But remember, these outcomes are merely beneficial by-products, not the main aim. If you start defusing thoughts or images with the aim of getting rid of them, then you're not truly accepting them. Rather, you're trying to use an acceptance strategy as a control strategy—and ultimately, that will backfire. So use the techniques in the way they were intended and for the right reasons, and they'll help keep you free of the happiness trap. And they'll also help you to face the . . .

9

Demons on the Boat

Imagine you're steering a ship far out at sea. Below the deck, out of sight, lies a vast horde of demons, all with enormous claws and razor-sharp teeth. And they've made a deal with you: as long as you keep the ship drifting aimlessly out at sea, they'll stay beneath the deck, so you don't have to look at them. But if you ever start heading toward the shore, they immediately rush up on deck, flap their wings, bare their fangs, and threaten to tear you to shreds. Not surprisingly, you don't like that very much, so you say: "Sorry demons! I didn't mean it! Please, go back down below." And you turn the ship around and drift back out to sea, and the demons disappear beneath the deck. So you breathe a sigh of relief, and everything seems okay—for a while.

The problem is, you soon get fed up of drifting aimlessly. You get bored, lonely, miserable, resentful, and anxious. You see all those other ships heading toward the shore, and you know that's where you *really* want to be going. So one day, you pluck up courage, turn the tiller, and head toward the shore once again. But the moment you do, those demons swarm up onto the deck and threaten to rip you into pieces again.

But here's the interesting thing: although these demons are very good at threatening you, they never actually cause you physical harm. Why not? Because they can't! All they can do is growl loudly, wave their claws, and look terrifying—physically they can't even touch you. The only power they have is the ability to intimidate. So if you believe they're *really* going to do what they say they'll do, then they've got control of the boat.

But once you realize they have no capacity to physically harm you—then you're free. You can take your ship wherever you want—as long as you're willing to accept the demons' presence. All you have to do to reach land is let the demons gather round, let them scream at you all they like, and keep steering the ship toward the shore. The demons may howl and protest, but they're powerless to stop you.

However, if you're not willing to allow these demons on board, if you've got to keep them down below no matter what, then your only option is to stay adrift at sea. (Of course, you can try to throw the demons overboard, but while you're busy doing that no one is steering the ship, so you run the risk of crashing into rocks or capsizing. Besides which, it's a struggle you could never win, because there's an infinite number of those demons in the hold.)

"But that's horrible!" you may well protest. "I don't want to live surrounded by demons!" Well, I'm sorry to be the bearer of bad news, but you already are: they're called thoughts, feelings, memories, urges, and sensations. And those demons will keep showing up again and again, as soon as you start to take your life in a valued direction. Why so? Again, it all stems back to evolution. Remember, the mind of our ancestors had one overriding imperative: "Don't get killed!" And an important factor in not getting yourself killed is to get to know your environment. The better you know the terrain and the local wildlife then, obviously, the safer you are, whereas venturing into unknown territory exposes you to all sorts of exotic dangers. So if one of our ancestors decided to explore a new area, his mind would go into a state of red alert. "Look out!" "Be careful!" "Could be a crocodile in that lake!" And thanks to evolution, our modern minds do the same, only far more extensively.

Thus, as soon as we start to do something new, our mind will start warning us: "You might fail," "You might make a mistake," "You might get rejected." It warns us with negative thoughts, disturbing images, bad memories, and a wide range of uncomfortable feelings and sensations. And all too often we let these warnings stop us from taking our lives in the direction we really want. Rather than sail for shore, we drift at sea. Some people call this "staying in your comfort zone," but that's not a good name for it because the comfort zone is definitely not comfortable. It should be called the "misery zone" or the "missing-out-on-life zone."

In later chapters, when we start focusing on your values and on taking action to change your life for the better, these demons are going to challenge you. Depending on the nature of your current problems, you may choose to pursue a new career, start a new relationship, make some new friends, improve your physical fitness, or engage in some challenging project like writing a novel, taking a course, or enrolling in higher education—and what I guarantee you is this: whatever meaningful changes you start to make in your life, those demons will rear their ugly heads and try to discourage you.

That's the bad news.

Now here's the good news: if you keep steering your ship toward shore no matter how much the demons threaten you, many of them will realize they're having no effect and will give up and leave you alone. As for the ones that remain, after a while you'll get used to them. And if you take a good, long look at them, you'll realize they're not nearly as scary as they first appeared. You'll realize they've been using special effects to make themselves look a lot bigger than they really are. Sure, they'll still look ugly—they won't turn into cute, fluffy bunny rabbits—but you'll find them much less frightening. (And some of them will even turn out to be your friends.) What's more, you'll find that you can let them hang around without being bothered by them. And as you do that, you'll realize there's a lot more in your life than just those demons. There's all that sea and sky out there; there's sun on your face and a breeze in your hair; and there are dolphins, whales, seagulls, penguins, and flying fish. (And who knows? Maybe you'll even encounter a few mermaids!)

So one of my main aims in this book is to help you see through the special effects of your demons, to see them as they really are, so that they no longer intimidate you. We've already started to do this with thoughts and images, and next we're going to do it with emotions. But before moving on, take a few moments to think about the changes you'd like to make in your life. Ask yourself:

1. How would I act differently if painful thoughts and feelings were no longer an obstacle?
2. What projects or activities would I start (or continue) if my time and energy weren't consumed by troublesome emotions?

3. What would I do if fear were no longer an issue?
4. What would I attempt if thoughts of failure didn't deter me?

Please take at least ten minutes to think about these questions. Better yet, write down your answers for future reference.

• • • • •

When you contemplate these four questions, what troublesome thoughts and images appear? Do you visualize yourself getting hurt in some way? Does your mind tell you, "It's hopeless" or "It's too hard" or that you can't make these changes because you are too weak/inadequate/depressed/anxious/stupid/unlovable?

Write a list of these troublesome thoughts and images and once you've done it, set aside five minutes a day to practice defusing them. (And when your mind makes up some excuse for not practicing, please remember to thank it!) As I've said several times before, practice is the key to success. The more you can see these thoughts for what they are — nothing more than words and pictures — the less influence they will have over your life. (To help motivate yourself, you can download a "defusion practice sheet" from the resources page on www.thehappiness trap.com.)

Defusion is a big topic, and we'll be coming back to it at later stages. But now, for the next few chapters, we'll look at how to handle painful feelings. Which seems to beg the question . . .

10

How Do You Feel?

If you were trekking through the Alaskan wilderness and you suddenly came face to face with a huge grizzly bear, what would you do? Scream? Call for help? Run away? We'll return to that later, after we've answered this one: What *are* emotions?

Scientists have a hard time reaching any kind of consensus on what emotions actually are, but most experts agree on three things:

1. Emotions originate from the middle layer of the brain, known as the "midbrain."
2. At the core of any emotion is a complex series of physical changes throughout the body.
3. These physical changes prepare us to take action.

Physical changes in the body may include alterations in heart rate, blood pressure, muscle tone, circulation, and hormone levels, as well as the activation of different parts of the nervous system. We notice these changes as sensations, such as "butterflies" in the stomach, a "lump" in the throat, watering eyes, or clammy hands. We also notice them as urges to act in a particular way, such as to cry, laugh, or hide.

Emotions influence us to act in different ways. For example, under the influence of any strong emotion, we commonly make changes to our voice, facial expression, body posture, and behavior. The likelihood that we will act in a particular way when experiencing a particular emotion is known as an "action tendency." But notice the key word here:

tendency. A tendency means we have the inclination to do something; it doesn't mean we have to do it, that we have no choice. It just means we *tend* to act that way. So, for example, if you're anxious about running late, you may have the tendency to drive above the speed limit, but you can still choose to drive legally and safely if you wish. Or if you're angry with someone, you may have a tendency to yell at them, but you can choose to talk calmly if you wish.

To understand what constitutes an emotion, let's take a look at anxiety. The experience of anxiety varies from person to person (as does any emotion), but it may include some or all of the following:

- physical changes such as raised blood pressure, increased heart rate or perspiration, or a faster rate of breathing
- sensations such as a racing heart, churning stomach, trembling legs, shaking hands, or sweaty palms
- urges to run away or to quit what you're doing
- action tendencies such as fidgeting, talking rapidly, or pacing up and down (People often notice this action tendency as an "urge.")

Emotions are closely tied up with thoughts, memories, and images. For instance, when you're feeling afraid, you may have thoughts about what might go wrong, memories of other times you've felt afraid, or mental images of anything from a car crash to a heart attack.

Do Our Emotions Control Our Behavior?

The answer to this is, quite simply, no! Our emotions definitely do not control our behavior. For example, you can feel angry but act calmly. You may have the tendency to shout, grimace, clench your fists, or lash out physically or verbally, but you don't have to. You can, if you choose, speak slowly and calmly, maintain a look of serenity on your face, and hold your body in an open, relaxed posture.

I'm sure that at some point in your life you have felt afraid, yet you persisted in the face of that fear even though you felt like running away.

In other words, you had a tendency to run, but you chose not to. We all have experienced this, for instance, when taking a test, asking someone for a date, going for a job interview, speaking before a group, or partici-pating in a dangerous sport.

You already know that whenever I give a speech in public I experi-ence anxiety. And yet, when I reveal this to my audience (as I usually do), they are always amazed. "But you look so calm and confident," they say. That's because even though I'm *feeling* anxious (racing heart, churning stomach, sweaty palms), I am not *acting* anxiously. Anxiety typically gives us the tendency to fidget, breathe rapidly, or talk fast; yet I do the very opposite of these things. I consciously choose to talk slowly, breathe slowly, and move slowly. The same is true for virtually all pub-lic speakers. Even after years of experience, they still commonly feel anxious, but you'd never know it, because they act calmly.

Now let's return to your trek through the Alaskan wilderness. If you suddenly come face to face with a grizzly bear, then obviously, you will feel intense fear. And undoubtedly you'll feel the urge to turn and run. But if you've read your survival manual, you'll know that if you turn and run, you will incite the bear's pursuit instinct. It will chase after you, easily outrun you, and hey, presto, you're snack food. What you need to do is back away slowly, make no sudden moves or loud noises, and never turn your back on the bear.

Many people have survived by following this advice. They all felt terrible fear—that much was out of their control—but they were able to control how they acted. So here's the point I'm trying to hammer home: although you don't have much direct control over your feelings, you can directly control your actions. This realization will have important practical applications later because when it comes to making impor-tant changes in your life, it's far more useful to focus on what you *can* control rather than on what you can't.

The idea that emotions control your actions is a very powerful illu-sion. Psychologist Hank Robb compares this illusion to that of a sunset. When we watch a sunset, the sun appears to be sinking below the hori-zon. But in fact, the sun is not moving at all. It's the earth that's rotating away from it. And even though we've all learned this at school, it's so easy to forget! When you're watching that sun "sink below the horizon," it's almost impossible to believe that it's really stationary.

When we're feeling strong emotions, we may do all sorts of things we later regret. We may smash things, shout, abuse people, drink excessively, or engage in any number of destructive behaviors. And it seems as if the emotion were causing us to do this. But actually, it's not. We're only acting this way because we've developed bad habits. But if we consciously bring our awareness to how we are feeling and consciously observe how we're behaving, then no matter how intense our emotions are, we can still control our actions. Even when you're furious or terrified, you can stand up or sit down, close your mouth, drink a glass of water, answer the telephone, go to the toilet, or scratch your head. You can't stop yourself from feeling angry or afraid, but you certainly can control how you behave.

What about those cases where people get paralyzed by fear? It's true that in very rare instances, when people find themselves in a genuinely life-threatening situation, they may become temporarily "paralyzed" by fear, rather like a rabbit frozen in the headlights. But 99.9 percent of the time when we talk about being "paralyzed by fear," it isn't the literal truth. It's just a metaphor; a colorful turn of phrase. The person is not truly physically incapable of taking action; he or she is simply choosing not to.

Emotions Are Like the Weather

Emotions are like the weather—they're always present and constantly changing. They continually ebb and flow, from mild to intense, pleasant to unpleasant, predictable to utterly unexpected. A "mood" refers to the general tone of emotion across a period of time. A "feeling" refers to a discrete episode of emotion with distinctive, recognizable characteristics. Thus a "bad mood" is like an overcast day, but a feeling of anger or anxiety is like thunder or a shower of rain. We're always experiencing emotion of some sort (just as there is always weather of some sort). However, sometimes it isn't strong or distinct enough for us to describe it easily. At such times, if someone asks us how we're feeling, we might say "fine" or "I'm not feeling anything in particular."

The Three Phases of Emotion

There are three phases in the creation of an emotion.

Phase One: A Significant Event   An emotion is triggered by some sort of significant event. This event may happen inside of you (a distressing memory, a painful sensation, or a disturbing thought) or it may happen in the world around you (something you see, hear, smell, taste, or touch). Your brain notices this event and alerts you that it's important.

Phase Two: Getting Ready for Action   The brain starts to evaluate this event: "Is it good or bad? Beneficial or harmful?" At the same time, the brain starts to arouse the body for action: either to approach or to avoid the event. In this phase there is no distinctive "feeling" in the usual sense of the word. If the brain judges the event as harmful, the "fight-or-flight response" is triggered (I'll discuss this in detail in a moment), and our body prepares to either attack or escape. If the brain judges the event as potentially helpful, our body prepares to approach and explore it.

Phase Three: The Mind Gets Involved   In the third phase, as our body gets ready for action, we experience a variety of sensations and impulses, and our mind starts attaching meaning to those changes. At this point, we can recognize distinctive emotions such as frustration, joy, or sadness.

The Fight-or-Flight Response

The fight-or-flight response is a primitive survival reflex that originates in the midbrain. It has evolved on the basis that if something is threatening you, your best chance of survival is either to run away (flight) or to stand your ground and defend yourself (fight). You heart rate speeds up, your body floods with adrenaline, blood shunts to the large muscles of your arms and legs, and your breathing increases to give you more oxygen, all of which primes you to flee or fight.

So whenever we perceive a threat, the fight-or-flight response immediately activates. In prehistoric times, this response was life saving. When a woolly mammoth charged you, if you couldn't escape, your only hope was to fight it. However, in this modern age, most of us rarely find ourselves in life-threatening predicaments, and the fight-or-flight response is often triggered in situations where it is of little or no use to us.

Once again, evolution is the culprit here. Our mind, trying to make sure we don't get killed, sees potential danger almost everywhere: in a moody spouse, a controlling boss, a parking ticket, a new job, a traffic jam, a long line at the bank, a big mortgage, an unflattering reflection in the mirror—you name it. The threat may even come from the mind itself in the form of a disturbing thought or image. Obviously, none of those things are actually life threatening, but our brain and body react as if they were.

If our brain judges an event as harmful, the fight-or-flight response is triggered, and it rapidly evolves into an unpleasant feeling such as fear, anger, shock, disgust, or guilt. If our brain judges the event as good or beneficial, we rapidly develop a pleasant feeling such as calm, curiosity, or happiness. The former feelings, we tend to describe as "negative." The latter feelings, we tend to describe as "positive." But actually, they're neither positive nor negative—they're all simply feelings.

"Well," you may be saying, "they may be simply feelings, but I much prefer the positive ones to the negative ones." Of course you do; so does everybody—it's human nature. But unfortunately, this preference often becomes so important to us that it leads to serious problems, contributing to something called . . .

11

The Struggle Switch

Have you ever seen one of those old cowboy movies where the bad guy falls into a pool of quicksand and the more he struggles, the faster it sucks him under? If you ever fall into quicksand, struggling is the worst thing you can do. What you're supposed to do is lie back, stretch out, keep still, and let yourself float on the surface. (Then whistle for your horse to come and rescue you!) This takes real presence of mind, because every instinct in your body tells you to struggle; but the more you struggle, the worse your situation becomes.

The same principle applies to difficult feelings: the more we struggle with them, the more trouble we create for ourselves. Now, why should this be? Well, imagine that at the back of your mind is a switch — we'll call it the "struggle switch." When it's switched on, it means we're going to struggle against any physical or emotional pain that comes our way; whatever discomfort we experience, we'll see it as a problem and try hard to get rid of it or avoid it.

Suppose the emotion that shows up is anxiety. If our struggle switch is ON, then that feeling is completely unacceptable. So we could end up with anger about our anxiety: "How dare they make me feel like this!" Or anxiety about our anxiety: "This can't be good for me. I wonder what it's doing to my body." Or guilt about our anxiety: "I shouldn't let myself get so worked up! I'm acting like a child." Or maybe even a mixture of all these feelings at once. What all these secondary emotions have in common is that they are unpleasant, unhelpful, and a drain on our energy and vitality. And then we may get angry or anxious or depressed about that! Spot the vicious cycle?

Now imagine what happens if our struggle switch is OFF. In this case, whatever emotion shows up, no matter how unpleasant, we don't struggle with it. Thus, when anxiety shows up, it's not a problem. Sure, it's unpleasant and we don't like it, but it's nothing terrible. With the struggle switch OFF, our anxiety levels are free to rise and fall as the situation dictates. Sometimes they'll be high, sometimes low, and sometimes there will be no anxiety at all. But more importantly, we're not wasting our time and energy struggling with it.

Without struggle, what we get is a natural level of physical and emotional discomfort, depending on who we are and the situation we're in. In ACT, we call this "clean discomfort." There's no avoiding "clean discomfort"; life serves it up to all of us in one way or another. But once we start struggling with it, our discomfort levels increase rapidly. And all that additional suffering we call "dirty discomfort."

Our struggle switch is like an emotional amplifier—switch it ON, and we can have anger about our anxiety, anxiety about our anger, depression about our depression, or guilt about our guilt. We could even have guilt about our anger about our anxiety—and then depression about that!

But it doesn't stop there. With our struggle switch ON, we are completely unwilling to accept the presence of these uncomfortable feelings, which means not only do we get distressed by them, we also do whatever we can to avoid or get rid of them. For some people, this means turning to drugs, alcohol, gambling, or food. Others may turn to TV, books, or computer games. Humans find an almost infinite number of ways to try to avoid or get rid of unpleasant feelings: from smoking to shopping, from sex to surfing the Internet. As we saw earlier, most of these control strategies are no big deal, as long as they're used in moderation. However, any of them is problematic if used excessively or inappropriately, readily leading to addictions, relationship issues, health problems, or just wasting time. All these secondary problems, and the painful feelings associated with them, fall under the heading "dirty discomfort."

With the struggle switch OFF:

- Our emotions are free to move.
- We don't waste time and energy fighting or avoiding them.
- We don't generate all that "dirty discomfort."

With the struggle switch ON:

- Our emotions are stuck.
- We waste a huge amount of time and energy struggling with them.
- We create a lot of painful and unhelpful "dirty discomfort."

Take the case of Rachel, a forty-three-year-old legal secretary. Rachel suffers from panic disorder, a condition characterized by sudden episodes of overwhelming fear: so-called panic attacks. During a panic attack the sufferer has an intense feeling of impending doom, associated with distressing sensations such as breathlessness, chest pain, a thumping heart, choking, dizziness, tingling in the hands and feet, hot and cold flushes, sweating, faintness, and trembling. This is a common disorder: according to the National Institute of Mental Health, roughly 6 million Americans experience panic disorders.

Rachel's major problem is actually her intense dislike of anxiety. She thinks anxiety is something terrible and dangerous, and she will do anything possible to avoid it. This means that as soon as she feels any sensation that remotely resembles anxiety, such as a racing heart or tightness in the chest, that sensation will itself trigger further anxiety. Then, as her anxiety level rises, those unwanted sensations grow even stronger. This in turn triggers even more anxiety, until soon she is in a state of full-blown panic.

Rachel's world is steadily shrinking. She now avoids drinking coffee, watching scary movies, or doing any physical exercise. Why? Because all these things make her heart beat faster, which can then set off the whole vicious cycle. She also refuses to ride in elevators or airplanes, drive on busy roads, visit crowded shopping centers, or attend large social gatherings. Why? Because she knows she might feel anxious in those situations, and anxiety is something she wants to avoid at any cost!

Rachel's case is extreme, but to a lesser extent we all do the same thing. All of us, at times, avoid challenges in order to escape the stress or anxiety that goes with them. And as I've said before, in moderation this is not a problem. But the more extensive that avoidance becomes, the more we start to suffer in the long run.

"Yes, that all makes sense," I hear you say, "but how can I stop struggling with difficult feelings when they feel so bad?" The answer is by using a simple technique called "expansion." But before we come to that, we need to explore . . .

12

How the Struggle Switch Developed

As you read through the emotions listed below, just notice, without thinking too hard about it, which ones you automatically judge as "good" or "positive," and which you automatically judge as "bad" or "negative."

- Fear
- Anger
- Shock
- Disgust
- Sadness
- Guilt
- Love
- Joy
- Curiosity

You have just read a list of the nine basic human emotions. Most people tend to automatically judge the first six emotions as "bad" or "negative" and the last three as "good" or "positive." Why is this so? It's largely because of the stories we believe about emotions.

Our thinking self loves to tell us stories, and we know how these stories affect us when we fuse with them. Here are some of the many unhelpful stories that our thinking self may tell us about emotions:

- Anger, guilt, shame, fear, sadness, embarrassment, and anxiety are "negative" emotions.

- Negative emotions are bad, dangerous, irrational, and a sign of weakness.
- Negative emotions will damage my health.
- People should hide their feelings.
- Expressing feelings is a sign of weakness.
- Strong emotions mean I'm out of control.
- Women shouldn't feel angry.
- Men shouldn't feel afraid.
- Negative emotions mean there's something wrong with my life.

You may agree with some or all of the above, or you may have beliefs that are quite different; it depends largely on your upbringing. If you grew up in a family where "positive" emotions were freely expressed but "negative" emotions were frowned upon, then you quickly learned that the "negative" ones were to be avoided. If your family tended to suppress or hide their feelings, then you learned to keep your feelings bottled up. If your parents believed in "getting anger off your chest," you may have learned that it's good to express anger. But if you were frightened by a parent's display of anger, you may have decided that anger is bad and should therefore be suppressed or avoided.

WHAT WAS YOUR CHILDHOOD PROGRAMMING?

It's a useful exercise to spend some time thinking about your childhood programming regarding emotions. This can often give you insight into how and why you struggle with certain feelings. Please take some time to write down answers (or at least think about them) to the following questions. As you were growing up:

- Which emotions were you told were desirable or undesirable?
- What were you told about the best way to handle your emotions?
- What emotions did your family freely express?
- What emotions did your family suppress or frown on?
- How did the adults in your family handle their own "negative" emotions?
- What emotional control strategies did they use?

- How did the adults in your family react to your "negative" emotions?
- As a result of all this programming, what ideas are you still carrying around today about your emotions and how to handle them?

Judging Our Emotions

One reason we tend to judge emotions as "bad" or "negative" is because they feel unpleasant; they create uncomfortable sensations in our bodies. We don't like those sensations, so we don't want them. On the other hand, we do like pleasant sensations, so naturally, we want more of them.

If you judge an emotion as "good," you'll probably try hard to get more of it; and if you judge it as "bad," you're apt to try even harder to get rid of it. Thus, judging sets you up for a struggle with your feelings. In ACT we encourage you to let go of judging your feelings altogether and to see them for what they are: a stream of constantly changing sensations and urges, continuously passing through your body.

Just because some sensations and urges are uncomfortable doesn't mean they're "bad." For example, if you grew up in a family where people didn't openly express love and affection, then you may find loving feelings uncomfortable. Does that mean they're "bad"? And isn't it interesting that many people judge fear a "bad" emotion, yet they will pay good money to watch a horror movie or read a thriller, precisely to experience that very feeling! So no emotion is in itself "bad." "Bad" is just a thought; a judgment made by our thinking self. But if we fuse with that thought—if we literally believe that the feeling is "bad"—then, naturally, we will struggle with it all the harder. (And we know where that leads.)

Any defusion strategy can help you deal with unhelpful thoughts about your feelings. For example, suppose your mind says, "This anxiety is terrible." You could then say to yourself, "I'm having the thought 'This anxiety is terrible.'" Or, more simply, you could say, "Thanks, Mind!"

One useful strategy for judgments is simply to label them. Each time you notice a judgment, you silently say to yourself, "Judging." Acknowledge its presence, recognize that it's only words, and let it be. The aim here is to *let go* of judgments; not to *stop* them. Your thinking self is an expert judge and will never stop judging for long. But you can learn to let go of those judgments, more and more, instead of getting caught up in them.

And what if the feeling really is "terrible"? Then we come back to the pragmatic approach: Is this thought helpful? If you fuse with the thought "This feels terrible!" will that help you deal with your emotions or will it simply make you feel worse?

How the Mind Adds to Our Emotional Discomfort

Judging is one of the most common ways our mind adds to our emotional discomfort; however, there are plenty of others. Below is a list of common questions the mind asks or comments that it makes that often stir up or intensify unpleasant feelings.

"Why Am I Feeling Like This?"

This question sets you up to run through all your problems one by one, to see if you can pinpoint what caused your feelings. Naturally, this just makes you feel worse, because it creates the illusion that your life is nothing but problems. It also leads to a lot of time lost in unpleasant thoughts. (And does this process help you in any practical way? Does it help you take action to change your life for the better?)

People generally ask this question because they think if they can figure out why they're feeling so "bad," they'll be able to figure out a way to feel better. Unfortunately, this strategy almost always backfires, as above. And more to the point, in most cases it doesn't really matter that much exactly *why* these unpleasant feelings arose; what matters is how you respond to them. The basic fact is always this: what you are feeling is what you are feeling! So if you can learn how to accept your feelings without having to analyze them, you'll save yourself a lot of time and effort.

"What Have I Done to Deserve This?"

This question sets you up for self-blame. You rehash all the "bad" things you've done, so you can figure out why the universe decided to punish you. As a result, you end up feeling worthless, useless, bad, or inadequate. (And again, does this help you in any practical way? Isn't this just another ineffective control strategy?)

"Why Am I Like This?"

This question leads you to search through your entire life history looking for the reasons why you are the way you are. Frequently this leads to feelings of anger, resentment, and hopelessness. And it very often ends in blaming your parents. (And does this help you in any practical way?)

"I Can't Handle It!"

Variations on this theme include "I can't stand it," "I can't cope," "I'm going to have a nervous breakdown," and so on. Your mind is basically feeding you the story that you're too weak to handle this, and something bad is going to happen if you keep feeling this way. (And is this a helpful story to pay attention to?)

"I Shouldn't Feel Like This."

This is a classic. Here your mind picks an argument with reality. The reality is this: the way you are feeling right now is the way you are feeling. But your mind says, "Reality is wrong! It's not supposed to be this way! Stop it! Give me the reality I want!" This kind of argument with reality never ends in your favor. And does it change anything?

"I Wish I Didn't Feel Like This!"

Wishful thinking: one of the mind's favorite pastimes. ("I wish I felt more confident." "I wish I didn't feel so anxious.") This can keep us wrapped up in second-guessing ourselves for hours, imagining how our lives could be so much better if only we felt differently. (And does this help us deal with the life we have now?)

And the list could go on and on. Suffice to say, the thinking self has lots of ways either to directly intensify our bad feelings or else to get us to waste a huge amount of time uselessly brooding on them. So from now on, catch your mind in the act when it tries to hook you with these questions and comments. Then simply refuse to play the game. Thank your mind for trying to waste your time and focus instead on some useful or meaningful activity. You may find it helpful to say, "Thanks, Mind, but I'm not playing today."

The Struggle Switch Revisited

Now you can see how the struggle switch got there. Our thinking self created it by telling us that uncomfortable feelings are "bad" or "dangerous," that we can't cope with them, that we are defective or damaged for having them, that they will take over or overwhelm us, or that they will harm us in some way. If we fuse with these stories, the switch goes ON and we perceive uncomfortable emotions as a threat. And how does our brain respond to a threat? It activates the fight-or-flight response, which then gives rise to a whole new set of unpleasant feelings.

To draw an analogy, suppose a distant relative shows up on your doorstep. You've never met this relative before, but you've been told a lot of stories about her. You've been told that she's bad, that she's dangerous, that no one can stand her, that the only relationships she has are with defective or damaged people, and that she always ends up hurting or damaging those people or taking control of them and ruining their lives.

If you truly believed those stories, what would your attitude be toward this relative? Would you want her in your house? Would you want her anywhere near you? Of course not. You'd do anything you could to get rid of her as fast as possible. But what if all those stories were false or exaggerated? What if this relative were actually an okay person who had just been the victim of malicious gossip?

The only way you'd ever find out would be to spend some time with her, put aside all the gossip and slander, and check her out for yourself. You've probably already experienced something like this in your own life. Perhaps there was once someone at school or at work whom you'd heard a lot of bad things about. Then you spent some time with them and discovered they were nowhere near as bad as their reputation.

And so it is in learning to handle unpleasant emotions; what you need to do is have a direct experience of them, to connect with them directly via your observing self, rather than automatically believing the stories of your thinking self. When you do this, you'll discover that those feelings are nowhere near as bad as you thought, and you'll realize they can't possibly harm you, control you, or overwhelm you.

Sometimes when I say, "Your emotions can't harm you," people mention the research that shows that chronic anger and depression can have bad effects on your physical health. However, the key word here is "chronic," which means ongoing, over a long period of time. Painful emotions become chronic only when you keep the struggle switch ON. Once you stop struggling, they are free to move, and they generally do so fairly quickly. So when you respond to your emotions with acceptance, they don't become chronic, and therefore they don't hurt you. Acceptance breaks the vicious cycle of struggle and frees you to invest your time and energy in life-enhancing activities. Which is why, in the next chapter, we're going to spend a fair bit of time on . . .

13

Staring Down Demons

How would you feel if the two people you loved most in the world suddenly died? Hard to imagine, isn't it? Even to think about it feels uncomfortable.

Earlier I mentioned Donna, whose husband and only child both died in a car crash. Most of us can't even begin to imagine her pain, but we can certainly understand her desire to avoid feeling it. When Donna came to see me six months after the accident, she was trying to avoid her pain by any means possible. This included drinking two bottles of wine each day, as well as taking a lot of Valium. Yet her pain was only increasing. Her "clean discomfort" (the natural pain of loss and grief) was compounded by a lot of "dirty discomfort" (all the additional suffering caused by her alcohol and drug problems). Learning the skill of "expansion" was an essential part of her recovery from this trauma.

So why the term "expansion"? Well consider some of the words we commonly use to describe feeling bad; words such as "tension," "stress," and "strain." If you look up these terms in a dictionary, you'll find they are all interlinked: tension is a state of being stretched or strained; stress is to subject to strain or pressure; and strain is to stretch beyond the proper point or limit. All these words imply that our feelings are too big; they are pulling us apart and stretching us beyond our limits. Contrast these terms with "expand": to increase in extent, size, volume, scope; to spread, unfold, or develop.

Basically, expansion means making room for our feelings. If we give unpleasant feelings enough space, they no longer stretch or strain us.

Typically, when unpleasant emotions arise, we "tense up"; that is, our muscles tighten and contract. It's as if we were trying to squeeze these feelings out, to push them out of our body by sheer brute force.

With expansion, we're intending the very opposite. Instead of squeezing down, we're opening up. Instead of increasing tension, we're releasing it. Instead of contracting, we're expanding.

We also commonly talk about being "under pressure" and of needing "room" or "breathing space." It's exactly the same when it comes to our own feelings: if we feel "pressure" building, we need to give them space. Fighting or avoiding our feelings does not create room for them; expansion does.

When you hear the term "expanse of water" or "expanse of sky," what comes to mind? Most people imagine a vast, open space. This is what we are aiming for in expansion: to open up to our feelings and make plenty of room for them. This will ease the pressure, lighten the tension, and free those feelings to move. Sometimes they will move very rapidly; sometimes they will move more slowly. But as long as we make room for them, they will move. And more importantly, expansion frees us to invest our energy in creating a better life, rather than wasting it in useless struggles.

"Hang on a minute," you may say, "if I make room for these emotions, they'll ride roughshod over me—I'll lose control!" Though this is a common fear, it isn't based in fact. Remember, ACT has been proven effective with a wide range of psychological problems, from anxiety and depression to addiction and even schizophrenia. So if your thinking self is telling you scary stories, simply thank it.

The Two Selves Revisited

The process of expansion primarily involves the observing self, not the thinking self, so let's just take a moment to recap their differences. The thinking self is responsible for thinking, in the broadest sense of the word; it produces all our thoughts, judgments, images, fantasies, and memories, and it is commonly called "the mind." The observing self is responsible for awareness, attention, and focus. It can observe thoughts, images, memories, etc., but it cannot produce them. It has no commonly used word to describe it. (The closest terms in the English language are "aware-ness" or "consciousness.")

The following exercise will help distinguish these two distinct parts of you and will also give you a sense of something called "body aware-ness" (a key factor in expansion).

BODY AWARENESS

In the exercise that follows, you will be repeatedly asked to notice some-thing. In each case, take about ten seconds to do the noticing before you read on.

- Notice your feet.
- Notice what position your legs are in.
- Notice the position and curvature of your spine.
- Notice the rhythm, speed, and depth of your breathing.
- Notice the position of your arms.
- Notice what you can feel in your neck and shoulders.
- Notice your body temperature and which parts of your body feel warmest and coolest.
- Notice the air on your skin.
- Scan your body from head to toe and notice if there's any stiff-ness, tension, pain, or discomfort anywhere.
- Scan your body from head to toe and notice if there are any pleasant or comfortable sensations.

• • • • •

Hopefully, during that exercise you experienced that *awareness* of the body is very different from *thinking* about it. Awareness arises from the ob-serving self, and thoughts arise from the thinking self. Of course, some thoughts about your body probably popped into your head. But the *aware-ness* — the *noticing* — is a fundamentally different process from *thinking*.

If you didn't experience this distinction between awareness and think-ing, do the above exercise again. And notice that while the thinking self is chattering away, the observing self is simply paying attention to your body. Notice, too, that there are brief moments (which may last less than a second) when the thinking self shuts up and the observing self can observe without any distraction.

Once you have experienced the distinction, it's time to move on to . . .

Expansion

In practicing expansion, we need to sidestep the thinking self—to let its unhelpful commentary fade into the background like a distant radio—and connect with our emotions through the observing self. This will enable us to experience our emotions directly, to see them as they actually are, rather than as the thinking self claims they are. According to the thinking self, negative emotions are giant, dangerous demons. However the observing self reveals them for what they are: relatively small and harmless (even if they're ugly).

So in practicing expansion, the aim is to *observe* your emotions, not *think* about them. There's just one problem: the thinking self never shuts up! This means that while you practice expansion, your thinking self will continually try to distract you. It may pass judgments on your feelings or try to analyze them or tell you scary stories about them or claim that you can't handle them. (Or it may say, "Don't bother with these exercises; reading about them is enough." It may even suggest that you "do them later," knowing full well that you probably won't.)

None of this needs to be a problem. Just allow those thoughts to be there and let them come and go as they please. Acknowledge their presence, but don't focus on them. Treat them as if they are cars driving past your house—you know they're there, but you don't have to peer out the window each time one goes by. And if a thought does hook you (in the same way that the sound of screeching tires might pull you to the window), then the moment you realize it, gently refocus on what you are doing.

This is essentially the same defusion skill as you learned in the Ten Deep Breaths technique in chapter 7 (page 67). If you haven't been regularly practicing that exercise, then *please,* start right now! Go back to chapter 7 (page 67), read through the Ten Deep Breaths exercise, then practice it at least ten times a day for a week before you read on any further. Remember, there's no great rush to "get through" this book. Think of it like a holiday—you get more out of it if you take your time, rather than trying to see all the sights in one day.

So, when practicing expansion, let your thoughts come and go in the background and keep your attention focused on your emotions. And remember:

- The essence of an emotion is a set of physical changes in the body.
- We primarily notice these changes as physical sensations.

Expansion starts with noticing what we're feeling in our body (body awareness) and observing precisely where those sensations are located. It then progresses to studying those sensations in more detail. This is the first of four basic steps, outlined below.

THE FOUR STEPS OF EXPANSION

The four basic steps of expansion are: observe your feelings, breathe into them, make room for them, and allow them to be there. Sounds simple doesn't it? That's because it is. It's also effortless. However, that does not mean it's easy! Remember the quicksand scenario? Lying back and floating on quicksand is both simple and effortless—yet it's far from easy. But don't worry. If you fell into quicksand several times a week, you'd soon be a pro at lying back and floating. And the same is true for expansion: the more you practice, the easier (and more natural) it becomes.

So let's take a look at these steps in a bit more detail, and then it's practice time. Whenever you're struggling with an unpleasant emotion of any sort, follow these four steps:

Step 1: Observe

Observe the sensations in your body. Take a few seconds to scan yourself from head to toe. As you do this, you will probably notice several uncomfortable sensations. Look for the one that bothers you the most. For example, it may be a lump in your throat, a knot in your stomach, or a teary feeling in your eyes. (If your entire body feels uncomfortable, then just pick the area that bothers you the most.) Now focus your attention on that sensation. Observe it with curiosity, like a scientist who has discovered some interesting new phenomenon. Notice where it starts and where it stops. If you had to draw an outline around this sensation, what shape would it have? Is it on the surface of the body, or inside you, or both? How far inside you does it go? Where is it most intense? Where is it weakest? How is it different in the center from around the edges? Is there any pulse or vibration? Is it light or heavy? Moving or still? Warm or cool?

Step 2: Breathe

Breathe into and around the sensation. Begin with a few deep breaths (the slower the better) and make sure you fully empty your lungs as you breathe out. Slow, deep breathing is important because it lowers the level of tension in your body. It won't get rid of your feelings, but it will provide a center of calm within you. It's like an anchor in the midst of an emotional storm: the anchor won't get rid of the storm, but it will hold you steady until it passes. So breathe slowly and deeply and imagine your breath flowing into and around the sensation.

Step 3: Create Space

As your breath flows into and around the feeling, it's as if you are somehow creating extra space within your body. You open up and create a space around this sensation, giving it plenty of room to move. (And if it gets bigger, you give it even more space.)

Step 4: Allow

Allow the sensation to be there, even though you don't like it or want it. In other words, "let it be." When your mind starts commenting on what's happening, just say, "Thanks, Mind!" and come back to observing. Of course, you may find this difficult. You may feel a strong urge to fight with this feeling or push it away. If so, just acknowledge that urge. (Acknowledging is like nodding your head in recognition, as if to say,

"There you are; I see you.") Then bring your attention back to the sensation itself.

Remember: don't try to get rid of the sensation or alter it. If it changes by itself, that's okay. If it doesn't change, that's okay too. Changing or getting rid of it is not the goal. The goal is to make peace with it, to let it be even if you don't like it or want it.

You may need to focus on this sensation anywhere from a few seconds to a few minutes, until you completely give up the struggle with it. Be patient; take as long as you need. You're learning a valuable skill.

Then once you've done this, scan your body again and see if there's another bothersome sensation. If so, repeat the procedure with that one. You can do this with as many different sensations as necessary. Keep going until your struggle switch is completely OFF.

As you practice this technique, one of two things will happen: either your feelings will change or they won't. It doesn't matter either way, because this technique is not about changing your feelings — it's about accepting them. If you have truly dropped the struggle with this feeling, it will have much less impact on you, regardless of whether or not it changes.

Now It's Time to Practice!

So at last we come to the practical part. In order to practice expansion, you'll need to have some uncomfortable feelings to deal with. So bring to mind something that's currently a problem, something that worries, disturbs, or stresses you — the sort of problem that prompted you to pick up this book in the first place.

"What?" you're probably yelling. "Are you crazy? I don't want to make myself feel bad!"

Well, join the club. I don't know anyone who *wants* to feel discomfort. The idea here is to be *willing* to feel it. *Wanting* something means you actively *like* it. *Willingness* simply means that you're *allowing* it.

Why develop willingness? Because throughout your life uncomfortable feelings will arise. If you keep trying to avoid them, you'll simply create additional "dirty discomfort." By making room for your feelings and *willingly* feeling them (even though you may not *want* to), you'll change your relationship with them. They'll become much less threatening and will have much less influence on you. They'll also take up much less time and energy.

The more we turn away from our demons, the harder we try not to look at them, the bigger and scarier they seem. Menacing shapes half-glimpsed from the corner of our vision are far more disturbing than the things we can see clearly. That's why in horror movies, they always film the monster lurking in darkness. If they brought it out into broad daylight, it wouldn't be nearly as scary.

"But isn't this all a bit masochistic?" you may ask.

Well, if you were feeling pain just for the sake of it, then yes, that would be masochism. But this is not the case in ACT. We don't recommend exposing yourself to discomfort unless it's in the service of something important.

Suppose you get mild arthritis in your left ankle, so that from time to time it swells up and aches. And suppose your doctor offers to amputate your leg. There's no way you'd consent to that for something so minor, is there? But suppose you developed bone cancer in that leg, and amputation became your only chance of survival. Then you would certainly do it. You would accept the discomfort of amputation because it's in the service of something important: your life!

It's the same with emotional discomfort. There's no point in wallowing aimlessly in it. In ACT, accepting discomfort has only one purpose: to help you take your life forward in a meaningful direction. Thus, in bringing up some discomfort in order to practice expansion, you are learning a valuable skill for transforming your life.

So enough of the talk, already! It's time to take action. Once again, read through the four steps of expansion described above. Then bring to mind some major problem in your life and dwell on it for a minute or two in order to dredge up some unpleasant feelings.

Once you have a feeling to work with, practice the four steps: observe, breathe, create space, and allow. (This technique is one of several which I have recorded on CD, because many people find it much easier when a voice guides them through the process. For details, see the resources section at the end of this book.) When practicing this technique, it's important to have no expectations. Instead, simply notice what happens, and if you have any problems, don't be concerned. In the next chapter you'll learn how to resolve them.

14

Troubleshooting Expansion

I said it before and I'll say it again: to practice expansion may be simple, but it sure isn't easy. But then again, what meaningful challenge is? Raising kids, keeping fit, nurturing a relationship, developing a career, creating a work of art, caring for the environment: all these meaningful challenges involve some difficulty. So why should practicing expansion be any different? Like any new skill, it's difficult to begin with, but with practice, it gets easier. Below you'll find answers to common concerns and problems about expansion.

Frequently Asked Questions about Expansion

Q: I tried to make room for the feeling, but it was too overwhelming. What should I do?

A: Just pick *one* troublesome sensation and keep your focus on it. Aim to accept just that one sensation, even if it takes you several minutes. Once you've done that, go ahead and pick another one.

Q: It's hard to stay focused on one sensation.

A: Yes, sometimes it is hard—at first. But it gets easier with practice. Give it your best shot, and if your attention wanders to another sensation, then as soon as you realize it, bring it back again.

Q: But my thoughts keep distracting me.

A: Yes, this is the basic nature of the mind. It distracts you again and again, pulling you out of your experience. So when it starts chattering, just say, "Thanks, Mind!" or silently say to yourself, "Thinking," then gently return your attention to the sensation. Each time you do this, you are learning two valuable skills: first, to notice when you're all caught up in your thoughts (fusion), and second, to refocus your attention after it has wandered.

Q: That was fantastic. The moment I made room for my unpleasant feelings, they disappeared. Is this what I can expect every time?

A: No, no, no! When we practice expansion, unpleasant feelings often disperse rapidly. But (as with defusion techniques) this is merely a bonus, not the main intention. The aim with expansion is simply to make room for your feelings, to feel whatever you are feeling without a struggle. Often those feelings will move very rapidly, but sometimes they won't. So if you're expecting to "feel good," then sooner or later you'll get disappointed and end up struggling again.

Q: The feelings disappeared at first, but then they came back again.

A: Many uncomfortable feelings will surface repeatedly. If someone you love has died, then waves of sadness may keep washing over you for many weeks or months. And if you've been diagnosed with cancer or some other serious illness, waves of fear will surge up again and again. As the saying goes, "You can't stop the waves, but you can learn to surf."

Q: I made room for my feelings, but they didn't change.

A: Sometimes feelings change quickly, and sometimes they don't. You need to accept that they will change in their own good time, not according to your schedule.

Q: Okay. I've accepted my feelings. Now what?

A: Having accepted your emotions, choose an area of your life that is important to you and take effective action in line with your values.

Q: Why do you keep coming back to actions and values?

A: Actions are important because, unlike your thoughts and feelings, you have a lot of control over them. Values are important because they can guide you and motivate you through situations where your feelings might lead you off course. Acting in accordance with your own deepest values is inherently satisfying and fulfilling—even though it often forces you to face your fears.

Pleasant feelings such as satisfaction, joy, and love are natural by-products of living by your values. But they aren't the only ones. Other by-products include uncomfortable emotions such as fear, sadness, anger, frustration, and disappointment. You can't have just the pleasant feelings without all the others. That's why it's important to learn how to accept all your feelings—pleasant, neutral, and unpleasant.

Q: Lots of self-help approaches suggest that when we are feeling bad we should try things like taking a hot bath, listening to music, reading a good book, savoring a hot chocolate, getting a massage, walking the dog, playing a sport we love, spending time with friends, and so on. Are you suggesting we shouldn't try such activities?

A: This is similar to a question I answered in chapter 2 (page 19). I'm sure you've had plenty of great advice from all sorts of sources about helpful activities to try when you're feeling "bad." And most of these activities can be deeply satisfying—as long as you genuinely value them; that is, as long as you engage in them out of a sense that they are truly meaningful to you. But if you do these activities mainly to run away from unpleasant feelings, they aren't likely to be all that rewarding—it's hard to appreciate life when you're trying to avoid something threatening.

Therefore, in ACT, acceptance always comes first. First you make room for your feelings and allow them to be exactly as they are. Then you ask, "What can I do right now that is truly meaningful or important?" This is very different from asking, "How can I feel better?" Then, once you've identified an activity you truly value, go ahead and take action.

You can remember these three steps with a simple acronym:

A = Accept your thoughts and feelings.
C = Connect with your values.
T = Take effective action.

Of course, once you fully accept your unpleasant feelings and immerse yourself in valued activities, pleasant feelings will often start to emerge. But as I've said countless times before, this is just a bonus, not the main goal. The main goal is to engage in meaningful activities, no matter how you feel. It is this that, in the long run, makes life fulfilling.

Q: I did accept my feelings for a little while, but then I started struggling with them again.

A: This is common. We often need to accept, accept, and accept again. The word "acceptance" is misleading, because it seems like a one-time action. In fact, acceptance is an ongoing process. A better word might be "accepting."

Q: What do I do if strong feelings come on when I'm at work or in some other situation where I can't just sit down and practice expansion?

A: With practice, expansion can happen almost instantly. It takes only a couple of seconds to take a slow, deep breath, scan your body, and make some room for what you're feeling. Once you've done that, focus your attention on effective action rather than getting caught up in your feelings.

Q: Is slow, deep breathing essential?

A: No, it's not. But most people find it very helpful. The other two steps, observing and allowing, are the only essential aspects of expansion.

Q: How can I accept my feelings when they have embarrassing side effects, such as making me blush!

A: In my days as a family doctor, I hated stitching up wounds on small children. The kids were usually terrified, and they screamed and bawled as their parents held them down. I felt like such a sadist! Often I felt quite anxious, and unfortunately my hands would start to shake. Now, obviously this was embarrassing, but if I got upset about it, they just shook all the more.

I didn't like my shaking hands, but I couldn't control them. It's just what my hands do when I get really nervous. (That's why I never became a bomb disposal expert!) So in these situations, the only sensible option was acceptance. I would say to the parents, "When I start stitching in a moment, you may notice my hands shaking a little. You don't need to worry. It always happens when I stitch up young kids. It won't stop me from doing a good job." Then, as I became involved in the stitching, my hands would gradually become steady. (Not always, mind you, but most of the time. And even on those few occasions when they kept shaking, it was much easier to deal with once I'd accepted it.)

Our bodies can do all sorts of awkward things when we have strong feelings. We may start to blush, twitch, shake, sweat, develop stomach cramps, lose an erection, fail to reach an orgasm, or even faint or vomit. Keep in mind that these reactions are often a result of the struggle switch being ON. With the switch ON, emotions are amplified (e.g., we get anxiety about our anxiety), and therefore the physical reactions in our body are greater. With the switch OFF, our emotions are smaller and change more rapidly, thereby causing less intense physical reactions. You're much better off if you accept these reactions than if you struggle with them. If you struggle, your feelings will intensify and your bodily reactions will worsen. However, often when we accept these reactions, they improve.

Remember, too, we're always talking about a twofold process: acceptance and action. So accepting these bodily reactions is the first step. Then, if something effective can be done about them, by all means do so. And if there is no effective remedy, acceptance is your best option.

Q: I'm starting to have my doubts about you. You sound like an anxious bundle of nerves.

A: ACT therapists don't go around pretending to be enlightened beings or to "have it all together." We freely admit that we're human, and we fall into the same traps as everyone else. So yes, you're absolutely right. I do experience a fair amount of anxiety in my life. But these days I generally handle it well. For example, when I am speaking publicly, I fully accept my anxiety without a struggle. (I'm no keener than the next guy to experience such feelings, but I'm completely willing to have them in order to do something I value.) Just before I start speaking, my anxiety skyrockets. Then, as I become increasingly involved in my talk, one of two things happens: either it goes down or it doesn't. Usually, it goes down fairly quickly, but even if it doesn't, it's not a problem, because now I fully accept it.

When I look back on my life, I can see how acceptance has dramatically reduced my anxiety levels. As a junior doctor, I was often in a state of anxiety, and as a consequence my hands were often sweaty. I then became increasingly anxious about my sweaty hands—and guess what happened? That's right. They became worse and worse until I developed a blistering sweat rash between my fingers. Nowadays my hands still get sweaty at times—but not often, because I don't worry about it. Looking back even further on my life, as a medical student I suffered terribly from social anxiety, and I drank extremely heavily to try to counteract it. As a consequence, I invariably got drunk and ended up doing stupid or outrageous things and waking up with a terrible hangover. These days I still get anxious in some social situations, but because I accept the anxiety, it comes and it goes, and it doesn't escalate in a vicious cycle. As a result, I get to enjoy social events without the unpleasant side effects of too much alcohol (which I now rarely drink).

Of course, there are times when I still handle my anxiety poorly, when I completely forget everything I've written in this book, and I pace up and down the house, worrying uselessly, or I wolf down an entire packet of Oreos. But as the years go by I do such things less and less frequently, and I get better and better at catching myself and doing something more effective instead.

The same will undoubtedly be true for you. You'll use these new skills at times and reap the rewards. And at other times you'll forget all about them. Again and again throughout your life, you will get caught up in a struggle with your feelings. That's the bad news. The good news is, the very moment you realize this has happened, you can instantly respond far more effectively!

Q: I don't really like all this acceptance stuff. Surely there must be easier ways of dealing with emotions.

A: You need to trust your own experience on this. ACT works particularly well with clients who have tried many different types of therapy or personal development programs. That's because these people have experienced for themselves that control strategies are not effective in the long run. So you may need to go and try some of the more popular approaches—hypnosis, visualization, affirmations, positive thinking, and so on—and discover for yourself that they really are not effective in the long term. Perhaps only then will you be fully ready to take on this approach. But before you go off and do that, reflect back to chapter 2 (page 19). Consider again all the ways you've tried to control "negative" thoughts and feelings, and ask yourself, did those methods work in the long term? And did they bring you closer to the life you want?

Q: Do these principles apply to all emotions?

A: Yes. But most of us have no problem with neutral or pleasant emotions. We only tend to struggle with the uncomfortable ones.

Q: I don't feel my emotions in my body. They're all in my head.

A: Sometimes it seems as though you don't feel emotions in your body, but everybody does. If you can't readily feel them, it suggests you're very disconnected from your body. If this is the case, practice the Body Awareness exercise (see chapter 13, page 99). Practice it for three or four minutes, twice a day, especially when you're feeling upset or stressed. Before long you'll be able to locate your feelings in your body. There are usually some key areas where we feel most intensely. Common ones include the forehead, temples, jaw, neck, shoulders, throat, chest, and abdomen.

Q: But I don't feel anything when I'm deeply upset; I just go numb.

A: Then practice accepting your numbness. Find the part of your body that feels the most numb and practice expansion around that. You'll usually find that as you make room for that numbness other uncomfortable feelings will arise. Then you can practice expansion around those.

Q: Can the thinking self assist with expansion?

A: Yes, it can. Although your thinking self naturally sets you up to struggle, it can also help you accept unpleasant feelings. It can help in two ways: acceptance self-talk and acceptance imagery.

ACCEPTANCE SELF-TALK

When practicing expansion, some people find self-talk very helpful. You may like to try saying things such as:

- "I don't like this feeling, but I have room for it."
- "It's unpleasant, but I can accept it."
- "I'm having the feeling of . . ."
- "I don't like it; I don't want it; I don't approve of it. But right here and now, I accept it."

True acceptance is not a thinking process. It's an attitude of openness, interest, and receptiveness, which originates with the observing self. Therefore, silently saying things such as the above examples will not make you truly accept (any more than silently saying, "I'm happy" will make you truly happy). But what these words can do is act as a prompt: they can remind us and guide us to accept.

ACCEPTANCE IMAGERY

This is a variation on the four-step expansion technique. It is often helpful for people who are good at visualizing. First scan your body and pick the sensation that bothers you the most. Observe it the way a curious scientist might. Now visualize that sensation as an object. What is the size and shape of it? Is it liquid, solid, or gaseous? Is it transparent or opaque? What color is it? Does the color vary? What is its temperature? Is it light, heavy, or weightless? How does the surface feel to the touch: rough, smooth, wet, dry, sticky, spiky, hot, cold? Is there any sound associated with it? Is there any vibration, pulsation, or movement within it? Is its position fixed or shifting?

Take a few slow, deep breaths. Breathe into and around this object. Create space for it. Open up around it and allow it to be there, to stay right where it is. You don't have to like it; just let it be. Don't try to get rid of the object and don't try to alter it. If it changes by itself, that's okay. If it doesn't change, that's okay, too. The aim is simply to accept it.

Repeat this with as many other sensations as you need to, until you have a sense of no longer struggling with these feelings.

Further Questions

Q: How much practice do I need to do?

A: Expansion is a very powerful acceptance skill, and obviously the more you practice, the better you get. So try it out with different feelings—both strong ones and mild ones. Use every opportunity. For example, if you're stuck in traffic, caught in a slow-moving line, or waiting for a friend who's running late, use that time to practice expansion. Notice what you're feeling in that moment: is it boredom, anxiety, irritation? Whatever it is, observe it, breathe into it, create space for it, and allow it (and if you wish, visualize it). At least then you'll be using your time constructively to develop a new skill, instead of merely struggling with your feelings.

Q: Isn't it unhealthy to keep focusing on unpleasant feelings?

A: I'm asking you to focus on your unpleasant feelings only to develop better acceptance skills. Obviously, in everyday life, focusing too much on your feelings will create problems; it will distract your attention from more important things. The ultimate aims of all this practice are:

- To be aware of your feelings, but not preoccupied with them
- To accept your feelings fully and allow them to come and go of their own accord
- To focus on your feelings if and when doing so would be helpful
- And *no matter what* you're feeling, to keep on doing what you value!

Q: So far we've focused only on dealing with sensations. How do I deal with urges?

A: By using a simple technique known as . . .

15

Urge Surfing

Emotions prime your body to take action, that is, every emotion gives you the impulse to act in a certain way. We call that impulse an "urge." In anger, we may feel the urge to shout, smash something (or someone), or just prove "I'm right, damn it!" In sadness, we may have an urge to cry, curl up into a ball, or have someone cuddle us. In fear, the urge may be to run away and hide, pace up and down, or talk too fast.

We also experience all kinds of urges *not* associated with emotions. For example, the urges to eat, drink, sleep, or have sex. Or the powerful urges of addiction: to gamble, smoke, drink, or take drugs. And when we don't feel too good, we often feel strong urges to use control strategies. For example, whenever I'm anxious, I get a strong urge to eat chocolate or go to the movies. In someone else, anxiety might trigger an urge to have a double scotch, smoke a cigarette, or go for a run.

To Act or Not to Act?

Whenever an urge arises, you have two choices: act upon it or don't act upon it. Therefore, once you are aware of an urge, you need to ask yourself, "If I act on this urge, will I be acting like the person I want to be? Will it help take my life in the direction I want to go?" If the answer is yes, then it makes sense to act on that urge. For instance, if you've been nasty to someone and you're feeling guilty, you may have an urge to apologize. If this is consistent with who you want to be and what you want to stand for, then it's sensible to go ahead and apologize.

On the other hand, let's suppose you've been nasty to someone and you're still feeling resentful toward them. In this case, rather than the urge to apologize, you may feel the urge to write them a nasty letter or say spiteful things about them to others. If this urge *isn't* consistent with who you want to be, then it's sensible *not* to act on it.

So when it comes to handling your urges effectively, the first step is simply to acknowledge what you're feeling. Just silently say to yourself, "I'm having the urge to do X."

The second step is to check in with your values: "Will acting on this urge help me be the person I want to be? Will it help me take my life in the direction I want?" If the answer is *yes*, then go ahead and act, using that urge to guide you and give you momentum. But if the answer is *no*, then instead take some action that's more in line with your values.

To exemplify this, let's take a look at Lisa, a twenty-one-year-old university student. Lisa values close relationships with her friends, and socializing with them regularly is an important part of her life. But when she feels depressed, she has the strong urge to stay at home, all by herself. (This is a very common urge with depressed moods.) So here we have the setup for a major conflict of interest. Lisa's values are pointing her in one direction (socializing), but the urge is pointing her in another direction (staying home alone). Which action is likely to take Lisa's life in the direction she wants: to act on her urge and stay home or to act in line with her values and go out and meet her friends?

Of course, it would be different if Lisa *truly valued* staying at home — if, for instance, she wanted to catch up on her studies for an important exam. If that were the case, staying home alone *would* be taking her life in the direction she wants, so it would make sense to act on the urge.

The Push and the Pull

So what do we do if an urge pushes us in one direction and our values pull us in another? We don't want to *struggle* with that urge because then it's hard to focus on effective action. So rather than try to resist, control, or suppress it, the aim in ACT is to *make room* for it, to give it enough time and space to expend all its energy — in other words, to practice *expansion*. And one marvelously useful technique for this is known as "urge surfing."

Have you ever sat on the beach and watched the waves? Just noticed them coming and going? A wave starts off small and builds gently. Then gradually it gathers speed and grows bigger. It continues to grow and move forward until it reaches a peak, known as a crest. Then, once the wave has crested, it gradually subsides. The same happens with urges in your body. They start off small and then steadily increase in size.

All too often we get into a struggle with our urges; that's why we talk of "resisting" them. In urge surfing, though, we don't try to *resist* our urges—we just give them space. If you give an ocean wave enough space, it will reach a crest and then harmlessly subside. But what happens if that wave encounters resistance? Ever seen a wave *crash* onto the beach or *smash* against the rocks? It's loud, messy, and potentially destructive.

So urge surfing is a simple but effective technique in which we treat our urges like waves and "surf" them until they dissipate. The term was coined back in the 1980s by psychologists Alan Marlatt and Judith Gordon, as part of their groundbreaking work with drug addiction. The same principles they used with addictive urges can be applied to *any* urge: whether it's an urge to stay in bed all day, to quit a course, to avoid a challenge, or to yell at someone we love.

URGE SURFING, STEP BY STEP

To surf an urge rather than be "wiped out" by it, all you need to do is:

1. Observe it: notice where you feel it in your body.
2. Acknowledge, "I'm having the urge to . . . X, Y, Z."
3. Breathe into it and make room for it. (And *don't* try to suppress it or get rid of it.)
4. Watch the urge as it rises, crests, and then falls again. (And if your mind starts telling you unhelpful stories, silently thank it.) It's often helpful to score the urge on a scale of 1 to 10. For example, "I'm having the urge to smoke, and it's now a 7." Keep

checking in on the urge, noticing whether it's rising, peaking, or falling.

Remember, no matter how huge that urge gets, you have room for it. And if you give it enough space, then sooner or later it will crest and then subside. So observe it, breathe into it, create space, and allow it.

5. Check in with your values. Ask yourself, "What action can I take right now—instead of trying to resist or control my urges—that will enhance my life in the long term?" Then whatever the answer is, go ahead and do it!

In other words, to manage your urges effectively, you need to ACT:

A = Accept your thoughts and feelings.
C = Connect with your values.
T = Take effective action.

It's All about Balance

We experience urges all day long, every day of our lives, and most of the time acting appropriately on them is no big deal. In ACT, we're concerned only with urges that get in the way of living a meaningful life. For example, I act on my chocolate urges fairly regularly, and it's not a problem. But if I acted on them *all the time*, I'd be the size of an elephant, and that would not be in line with my values on health. On the other hand, if I *never* acted on them, I'd be unnecessarily depriving myself of a simple but satisfying pleasure.

The point is, you need to find a healthy balance. Don't put ridiculous expectations on yourself, deciding that you're *never again* going to act on self-defeating urges. *Of course* you will—you're human. You'll screw up again and again over the course of your life. But here's the thing: the instant you are aware of what you're doing, you have a chance to do something more effective. And over time you'll get better and better at catching yourself earlier and earlier.

While urge surfing can be very helpful, like any skill, it requires practice. (Look, you had to know that was coming.) The best way to practice is to put yourself in a situation where you're likely to feel confronted by troublesome urges. But don't choose just *any* challenging situation; choose one that moves your life forward in a meaningful way.

During the next week, pick two or three difficult situations that naturally occur when you take your life in a valued direction. These situations could be anything: getting some exercise, attending a class, or attempting something new at work. Once you're in those situations, notice your urges, surf them, and stay fully engaged in what you're doing.

Of course, staying engaged in what you're doing can be tricky, especially when the thinking self starts mouthing off. That's why in the following chapters we're going to look at a process called "connection," which is all about engaging in and connecting with our experience (rather than getting caught up in our thoughts and feelings). But before we get to that, we need to pay a brief visit . . .

16

Back to the Demons

So here we are again, back on the boat with all those scary demons. But hopefully now you're starting to see them as they really are, starting to make peace with them, so you're free to steer the boat where you want.

Naturally, at times those demons will steer you off course. (Why "naturally"? Because you're a normal human being, not a saint, guru, or superhero.) But here's the exciting thing: the moment you realize your boat is headed in the wrong direction, you can instantly turn it back around. Instantly. All it takes is awareness.

Of course, you may be a long way from shore at the time. And in fact, that very thought is often one of the demons: "I'm so far away from achieving what I want in my life, what's the point in even trying?" Well, the point is, the instant you turn that boat toward shore, you're heading in the direction that you want, and that's so much more rewarding than drifting at sea!

GETTING TO KNOW YOUR DEMONS

In chapter 9 you listed some of your main demons in terms of thoughts and images. Now it's time to add feelings to that list. The first step is to read through the questions below, noticing what thoughts and feelings automatically come to mind.

- What are the major changes you'd make in your life, if difficult thoughts and feelings were no longer an obstacle?
- What projects or activities would you start or continue if your time and energy were not consumed by troublesome emotions?
- What would you do if fear were no longer an issue?
- If difficult thoughts and feelings were no longer an obstacle . . .
  - What sort of relationships would you build, and with whom?
  - What improvements would you make in your health and fitness?
  - What changes would you make in your work?

In reading through your list, you have probably already noticed a variety of unhelpful thoughts and unpleasant feelings. If you're experiencing those right now just by reading these questions, then you can be sure they're going to confront you later when we focus on taking action. So take a few minutes and write down answers to these questions (or at least spend a few minutes thinking about them):

- What demons can you expect to find clambering up on deck as you steer your boat in a valued direction?
- What feelings and sensations might possibly act as obstacles?
- What thoughts and images might possibly act as obstacles?

The next step is to make some time to practice defusion and/or expansion with these demons. What valued activities can you do in the next few days that will give you a chance to meet these demons, see them for what they are, and make peace with them? Set yourself a few goals: specify the time, the place, and the activity you'll do. Then engage yourself fully in that activity.

And if you have trouble with any of this, don't be discouraged. In the next few chapters you'll be learning another useful skill that will make a world of difference.

17

The Time Machine

"Where are you?" asked my wife, startling me. We were halfway through a meal at a Japanese restaurant, and for the past couple of minutes I hadn't heard a word that she'd been saying. Or to be more accurate, I had heard the words but hadn't consciously listened to them. "Where are you?" was an appropriate question, because even though I was there physically, mentally I was miles away. I'd been completely "carried off" by thoughts about a troublesome family matter.

We've all had this happen to us. We're in a conversation, nodding and listening, but we're not paying a bit of attention, because we're "off in our heads" thinking about what we've got to do later or dwelling on something that happened earlier. Often we can get away with this "fake listening," but sometimes, to our great embarrassment, we get caught.

The thinking self is constantly generating thoughts—after all, that's its job. But all too often those thoughts distract us from where we are and what we're doing in the moment. Ever been for a drive in a car and reached your destination with no real memory of the journey? Or thought you knew where you were going but ended up driving to the wrong place? That's because your attention wasn't on the road; it was on the activity of your thinking self (daydreaming, planning, worrying, problem-solving, remembering, fantasizing, and all the rest). And this is how we habitually go through most of our lives.

Have you ever been asked, "What did you do today?" and not been able to remember? Do you ever find yourself snacking on something without even realizing it? Or read an entire page of a book and realize you haven't taken in a single word?

We say we were "lost in thought," "distracted," or "preoccupied"— all terms that mean our attention is fixed on the products of our mind instead of on what we are doing right here and now. That is, our observing self is distracted by our thinking self.

The thinking self is rather like a time machine: it continually pulls us into the future and the past. We spend a huge amount of time worrying about, planning for, or dreaming of the future, and a huge amount of time rehashing the past. This makes perfect sense in terms of evolution. The "don't get killed" device needs to plan ahead and anticipate problems. It also needs to reflect on the past, to learn from it. But even when our mind is thinking about the here and now, it's generally being judgmental and critical, struggling against reality instead of accepting it. And this constant mental activity is an enormous distraction. For a huge part of every day, the thinking self completely diverts our attention from what we're doing.

Suppose you're trying to have a conversation with someone and you're giving most of your attention to thoughts like, "He thinks I'm boring" or "I've got to get my taxes done." The more attention you give to those thoughts, the less involved you are in the conversation. The same goes for everything you do, whether you're water-skiing or making love: the more you're engaged in your thoughts, the less you're engaged in the activity.

Of course, some activities require creative or constructive thinking as part of the process—playing chess, for instance, or doing a crossword puzzle. But even then thoughts can pull you away from what you're doing. If you're playing chess and carefully thinking through all your options, that's fine; those thoughts keep you involved in the game. But if you're giving your attention to thoughts like, "I'm going to lose," or "I wonder if that new Spielberg movie is out," those thoughts will pull you out of the game.

Now, obviously there are times when being absorbed in thought is precisely what you should be doing—for example, if you're dreaming up ideas for a new ad campaign, mentally rehearsing a speech, planning an important project, or simply solving a crossword puzzle. But too much of the time, we're so absorbed in our thoughts that we aren't fully engaged in our lives and aren't in touch with the wondrous world around us. And when we're like this, only half present with friends and family, we're not even connected with ourselves!

What Is Connection?

"Connection" means being fully aware of your here-and-now experience, fully in touch with what is happening in this moment. In practicing connection, we pull ourselves out of the past or the future and bring ourselves back to the present—right here, right now. Why do this? For three main reasons:

1. This is the only life you've got, so make the most of it. If you're only half present, you're missing out. It's like watching your favorite movie with sunglasses on or listening to your favorite music while wearing earplugs. To truly appreciate the richness and fullness of life, you have to be here while it's happening!
2. To quote the great novelist Leo Tolstoy, "There is only one time that is important: NOW! It is the most important time because it is the only time when we have any power." To create a meaningful life, we need to take action. And the power to act exists only in this moment. The past has already happened and the future doesn't exist yet, so we can only ever take action here and now.
3. "Taking action" doesn't mean just any old action. It must be effective action; action that helps us move in a valued direction. In order to act effectively, we need to be psychologically present. We need to be aware of what is happening, how we are reacting, and how we wish to respond.

This means we need to add three extra words to the "A" of ACT:

A = Accept your thoughts and feelings *and be present.*
C = Connect with your values.
T = Take effective action.

Connection is about waking up, noticing what's happening, engaging with the world, and appreciating the fullness of every moment of life. You've already experienced this many times in your life. Perhaps while on a walk in the countryside you feasted your eyes on the fields, the wildlife, and the trees and flowers, enjoyed the touch of a balmy summer breeze, and listened to the songbirds. Or during an intimate conversation with the one you love, you hung on their every word, gazed into their eyes, and felt the closeness between you. Or while playing with a child or a beloved pet, you were so involved in the fun of it all, you didn't have a care in the world.

As these examples suggest, connection often happens spontaneously in stimulating or pleasurable situations. Unfortunately, it rarely lasts for long. Sooner or later the thinking self pipes up, and its comments, judgments, and stories pull us out of the experience. And as for all those familiar, mundane, or unpleasant situations that make up a sizeable part of even the most privileged life, connection is minimal at those times.

Connection and the Observing Self

Connection happens through the observing self. It involves bringing our full attention to what is happening here and now without getting distracted or influenced by the thinking self. The observing self is by nature nonjudgmental. It can't judge our experience, because judgments are thoughts and therefore a product of the thinking self. The observing self doesn't get into a struggle with reality; it sees things as they are, without resisting. Resistance only happens when we fuse with our judgments that things are bad or wrong or unfair.

Our thinking self tells us that things shouldn't be as they are, that we shouldn't be as we are, that reality is in the wrong and our ideas in the right. It tells us that life would be better somewhere else or we would be happier if only we were different. Thus, the thinking self is often like a pair of dark goggles that dims and obscures our view of the world, disconnecting us from reality through boredom, distraction, or resistance.

The observing self, though, is incapable of boredom. It registers everything it observes with openness and interest. It's only the thinking self that gets bored, because boredom is basically a thought process: a story that life would be more interesting and more fulfilling if we were doing something else. The thinking self is easily bored because it thinks it already knows it all. It's been there, done that, seen the show, and bought the T-shirt. Whether we're walking down the street, driving to work, eating a meal, having a chat, or taking a shower, the thinking self takes it all for granted. After all, it's done all this stuff countless times before. So rather than help us connect with our present reality, it "carries us off" to a different time and place. Thus, when the thinking self is running the show, we spend most of our time only half awake, scarcely aware of the richness in the world around us.

The good news is that the observing self is always present and available. Through it we can connect with the vast length, breadth, and depth of human experience, regardless of whether that experience is new and exciting or familiar and uncomfortable. The fascinating thing is that when, with an attitude of openness and interest, we bring our full attention to an unpleasant experience, the thing we dreaded often seems much less bothersome than before. Likewise, when we truly connect with even the most familiar or mundane experience, we often see it in a new and interesting light. To experience this for yourself, try the following exercise.

CONNECTING WITH THIS BOOK

In this exercise the aim is to take a fresh look at the book in your hands, to see it with "new eyes." Imagine that you're a curious scientist and you've never seen an object like this before. Pick up the book and feel the weight of it in your hands. Feel the cover against your palms. Run your finger slowly down a page and notice the texture. Bring the open book to your nose and smell the paper. Slowly turn a few pages and notice the sound it makes. Look at the front cover of the book. Notice how the light reflects off the surface. Notice the shapes of the spaces between the words. Then turn to any page at random and notice the shapes of the white space surrounding the text.

• • • • •

How did you find that? You've been reading this book for quite a while and until now you've probably taken all these different aspects of it for granted. And the same is true for just about every aspect of our life. Over the next few chapters we're going to focus on several different aspects of connection, particularly how to use it when dealing with painful experiences. For the rest of this chapter, though, we're simply going to focus on "waking up": on connecting with the world around us and refocusing whenever we realize we have "disconnected."

A *Few Simple Connection Exercises*

In each exercise that follows, you'll be asked to connect with some experience, such as the sounds in your environment or the feelings in your body. When distractions in the form of thoughts and feelings occur:

- Let those thoughts and feelings come and go, and stay connected.
- When your attention wanders (and it will, I promise), the moment you realize it, acknowledge it.
- Silently say to yourself, "Thanks, Mind." Then gently bring your attention back to the exercise.

There are four short exercises, each lasting only thirty seconds, so there's no excuse for not doing them. It'll take two minutes to do them all!

CONNECTION WITH THE ENVIRONMENT

Once you've finished reading this paragraph, put the book down and notice your surroundings. Notice as much as you can about what you can see, hear, touch, taste, and smell. What's the temperature? Is the air moving or still? What sort of light is there and where is it coming from? Notice at least five sounds you can hear, at least five objects you can see, and at least five things you can feel against the surface of your body (such as the air on your face or your shoes around your feet). Put the book down now and do this for thirty seconds. Notice what happens.

AWARENESS OF THE BODY

As you're reading this paragraph, connect with your body. Notice where your legs and arms are and the position of your spine. Inwardly scan your body from head to toe; notice the sensations in your head, chest, arms, abdomen, legs. Put the book down, close your eyes, and do this for thirty seconds. Notice what happens.

AWARENESS OF THE BREATH

As you're reading this, connect with your breathing. Notice the rise and fall of your rib cage and the air moving in and out of your nostrils. Follow the air in through your nose. Notice how your lungs expand. Feel your abdomen push outward. Follow the air back out, as the lungs deflate. Put the book down, close your eyes, and do this for thirty seconds. Notice what happens.

AWARENESS OF SOUNDS

In this exercise, just focus on the sounds you can hear. Notice the sounds coming from you (from your breath and your movements), the sounds coming from the room, and the sounds coming from outside the room. Put the book down now, close your eyes, and do this for thirty seconds. Notice what happens.

• • • • •

So what did you notice? Hopefully, two things: First, that you are always in the midst of a sensory feast; you just don't usually realize it. Second, that it's very easy to get distracted by thoughts and feelings. To improve your ability to stay present and notice what is happening around you, practice the following two exercises on a daily basis.

NOTICE FIVE THINGS

This is a simple exercise to center yourself and connect with your environment. Practice it a few times every day.

1. Pause for a moment.
2. Look around and notice five objects you can see.
3. Listen carefully and notice five sounds you can hear.
4. Notice five things you can feel against the surface of your body.

You can develop this skill further by going for a daily walk and spending the whole time noticing what you can see, hear, smell, and physically feel (and refocusing whenever you realize you've been "disconnected").

CONNECTING WITH YOUR MORNING ROUTINE

Pick an activity that's part of your daily morning routine, such as brushing your teeth, combing your hair, or taking a shower. Totally focus on what you are doing, using all your five senses. For example, in the shower notice the various sounds of the water: as it sprays out of the nozzle, as it hits your body, as it gurgles down the drain. Notice the sensations of the water running down your back and legs. Notice the smell of the soap and the shampoo. Notice the clouds of steam billowing upward.

When thoughts and feelings arise, acknowledge their presence, let them be, and refocus on the shower. As soon as you realize that your attention has wandered off, thank your mind (or simply label it all "thinking") and refocus on the shower.

For starters, practice connecting with one part of your morning routine each day. Then, as your ability improves, extend it to other parts.

In the next three chapters we'll see how connection skills help us deal with painful life experiences. In the meantime, practice seeing the world through new eyes. And whenever you realize that the time machine has carried you off, bring yourself back to the here and now.

18

The Dirty Dog

When Soula turned thirty-three, her best friend organized a surprise birthday party in a local café. At first Soula was delighted, thrilled that all her closest friends and family had come together in her honor. But as the evening wore on she began to feel sad and lonely. When she looked around the room, her thinking self started telling her the "single and lonely" story. "Look at all your friends. They're all in long-term relationships or married and having kids, and you haven't even got a boyfriend! You're thirty-three now, for heaven's sake! Time's running out . . . Soon you'll be too old to have kids . . . Just look at them all, having so much fun . . . They don't know what it's like to go back to an empty apartment night after night . . . What's the point of celebrating? All you have to look forward to is being old, lonely, and miserable."

On and on it went, Radio Doom and Gloom, broadcasting at full volume. And the more Soula tuned in to it, the more she lost track of the party going on all around her. She hardly tasted the food, hardly heard the conversation. She became increasingly disconnected from the warmth, joy, and love that surrounded her.

Of course, it is true that Soula was single and getting older and that most of her friends were in long-term relationships. But remember the key question: Is this story helpful? In this case it clearly wasn't. And this was by no means an isolated episode. For most of a year now the "single and lonely" story had been a major source of misery for Soula, making her increasingly depressed.

Sadly, scenarios like this are all too common. The more we focus on unpleasant thoughts and feelings, the more we disconnect from the present moment. This particularly tends to happen with depression and anxiety. With anxiety you tend to get hooked by stories about the future, about things that might go wrong and how badly you're sure to handle them. With depression you tend to get hooked by stories from the past, about all the things that have gone wrong and how badly they've affected you. The thinking self then uses that history to convince you that the future is going to be just more of the same. These stories are very compelling, and we're all too ready to give them our full attention.

It's no surprise, then, that a common symptom of depression is anhedonia, which is the inability to take pleasure in previously enjoyable activities—after all, it's hard to enjoy what you're doing if you're not connected with it. But the reverse is also true: the more connected you are with a pleasurable activity, the more fulfilling it will be. Thus, connection is an important skill for getting the most out of life. As Soula practiced and improved her connection skills, she began to appreciate the good things she had in her life, instead of always focusing on what she lacked. And as a result, her depression lifted quite rapidly. (However I wouldn't want you to think this was some "quick fix" that transformed her life overnight. It was only the start of Soula's journey. We'll revisit her later in the book to see what else she did.)

Connection with Pleasant Experiences

To appreciate connection, practice it with at least one pleasant activity each day. Make sure it's a values-driven activity, not an avoidance-driven activity—that is, it's something you're doing because it's important, meaningful, or genuinely valued, and not just an attempt to avoid "bad feelings." The activity doesn't have to be anything mind-blowing. It can be something as simple as eating lunch, stroking the cat, walking the dog, listening to the birds, cuddling your kids, sitting in the sunshine, or listening to a favorite piece of music.

As you do this activity, pretend that this is the first time you've ever done it. Really pay attention to what you can see, hear, smell, touch, and taste. Savor every moment. And the moment you realize you've disconnected, thank your mind and refocus on what you're doing.

If it's hard to connect fully with pleasant events, then it's natural that we should so easily disconnect from the unpleasant ones. Whenever we encounter an unpleasant event, we naturally try our best to get rid of it or avoid it. But what if getting rid of it isn't our best option? What if this unpleasant situation is necessary for us to improve our quality of life?

For example, in order to maintain good health, you may at some stage need to have an operation, undergo some dental treatment, or practice some uncomfortable muscle-stretching routine. And to keep our finances healthy, most of us have to do a certain amount of budgeting and bookkeeping. If we want to live in a clean house, we may need to do a variety of unpleasant chores, and if we want a better job, we may need to attend some highly stressful interviews.

So why is connection helpful in these situations? First, it helps us turn OFF that struggle switch. The more we struggle against unpleasant situations, the more unpleasant thoughts and feelings we generate. Naturally, this only makes the situation worse. Secondly, when we really pay attention and we put aside the stories of the thinking self, we discover that these events just aren't as bad as we expected. You've probably already experienced this with expansion: when you observe unpleasant feelings with interest and openness, they're nowhere near as bad as they first seemed. Do I detect a note of scepticism? Then let me tell you about . . .

Washing My Dirty Dog

Recently I took my dog for a walk in the park and, he rolled around in the carcass of a dead bird. He loves to do disgusting things like that. Afterward he stank like . . . well, like a rotting carcass, so I had no choice but to bathe him. I had some very important matters to deal with that night, and I was frustrated that I had to waste my time on this unpleasant task. My mind was making all sorts of judgments: "Stupid dog! Why did you have to pick tonight to do something like this? Yuck! That smells disgusting!" And I was growing increasingly tense and irritable. But as I filled the tub with warm water, I realized that my struggle switch was ON, and I made the conscious choice to respond differently.

The fact was, no one else was going to wash the dog and I didn't want to leave him smelling like that. (Not that he would have minded.) I knew it would take about half an hour to wash him and dry him, so I figured I had a choice: I could spend that time stressed and irritable, disconnected from my experience, pressuring myself to finish as quickly as possible, while thinking about all the things I had to do afterward. Or I could connect with my experience and make the most of it. Either way, it would still take half an hour.

How do you make the most of washing a dirty dog? By being present and engaging in what is happening without judging it. So as I inhaled that foul odor I made room for my feelings of disgust and irritation. I allowed my unhelpful thoughts to come and go, and I focused on connecting through my five senses. I noticed the warm water on my hands and the reactions of my dog as I spoke to him gently. I focused with interest and openness on the feel of his wet hair, the smell of the shampoo, the changing color of the water, the sound of splashing, the movement of my arms, the movement of the dog, the movement of the water.

And I'd be lying if I said I enjoyed it. But the experience was much richer than on previous occasions when I rushed through it completely disconnected. And as a bonus, it was much less stressful for the two of us. However, as always, you should trust your own experience rather than what I say. Practice connecting with unpleasant, boring, or disagreeable tasks and notice what happens. And make sure that they're tasks you truly value; activities that serve to enhance your life in the long term. Following are some exercises to help you connect with the mundane activities in life.

CONNECTION WITH A USEFUL CHORE

Pick a chore that you don't like but that you know is helpful in the long run. It could be ironing clothes, washing dishes, cleaning out the car, cooking a healthy meal, bathing the kids, polishing your shoes—any task that you'd just as soon avoid. Then each time you do it, practice connection. Have no expectations; just notice what happens. For example, if you're ironing clothes, notice the color and shape of the clothing.

Notice the patterns made by the creases and their shadows. Notice how the patterns change as the creases disappear. Notice the hiss of the steam, the creak of the ironing board, the faint whispery sound of the iron moving over the material. Notice the grip of your hand on the iron and the movement of your arm and your shoulder.

If boredom or frustration arises, make room for it and refocus on what you're doing. When thoughts arise, let them be and go back to focusing on what you're doing. The moment you realize that your attention has wandered (and it will, repeatedly), gently thank your mind, briefly note what distracted you, and bring your attention back to what you're doing.

CONNECTION WITH A TASK
YOU'VE BEEN AVOIDING

Pick a task you've been putting off for a while. Set aside twenty minutes to make a start on it. During that time, focus completely on the experience. Connect with it fully, through the five senses, while making room for your feelings and defusing your thoughts. After twenty minutes, feel free either to stop or to continue. Do this for twenty minutes every day, until your task is completed.

Practicing connection is like building your muscles. The more you practice, the more strength you have to change your life. Many people fail to make important changes—changes that could significantly enhance their lives—because they're unwilling to accept the discomfort that accompanies change. For example, you may avoid changing to a more meaningful career because you don't want the discomfort of starting from scratch. Or you may avoid asking someone on a date because you don't want to risk rejection. The more you learn to connect, defuse, and expand, the less power you will give such discomfort to act as an obstacle. So aim two or three times a day to connect with both a pleasant valued action and an uncomfortable valued action. In the long run, the rewards will be well worth it.

19

A Confusing Word

It's time for us to take a little detour. In this chapter, we're going to look at the similarities and differences between ACT and other approaches to human suffering. But first we need to introduce and define a new word: "mindfulness." It's a slightly confusing word because it has nothing to do with having a "full mind." Different books will give you different definitions of "mindfulness," depending on their content. A spiritual or religious book will define it very differently from a book on sports psychology or effective leadership. So here's my definition: "mindfulness" means consciously bringing awareness to your here-and-now experience, with openness, receptiveness, and interest.

This definition tells us several things. Firstly, mindfulness is a conscious process; something we do deliberately. Secondly, it's not a thinking process; it's about awareness. Thirdly, it's about bringing our awareness to the present moment; in other words, paying attention to what's happening here and now. Fourthly, it's about doing this with a particular attitude: one of openness, interest, and receptiveness to our experience, rather than one of struggle, resistance, and avoidance.

When we practice mindfulness, we connect with the world directly, rather than being caught up in our thoughts. We let our judgments, complaints, and criticisms come and go like passing cars, and we fully engage in the present moment. When we are mindful of our own thoughts, we can see them for what they are and let them go. When we are mindful of our feelings, we can make room for them and let them be. And when we are mindful of our here-and-now experience, we are deeply connected with it. Thus defusion, expansion, and connection are all mindfulness skills.

So ACT is clearly a mindfulness-based therapy, and the purpose of this chapter is to point out the significant differences between ACT and other mindfulness-based approaches.

ACT Is about Taking Action

ACT is based firmly in the tradition of behavioral psychology: a branch of science that seeks to understand, predict, and influence human behavior. A major concept in ACT is the idea of "workability." (It's a concept I've been referring to throughout this book, but I haven't given it a name until now.) The workability of any given behavior means how well it works in the long run toward creating a rich and meaningful life. In ACT, we learn mindfulness skills to assist us in taking action to improve our life. We do not practice mindfulness in order to enter some mystical state or to get in touch with a higher truth. In any given circumstance, if defusion, expansion, and connection can help you act effectively, then it makes sense to practice them. Conversely, if they don't help you, then don't use them! The bottom line is always the same: does this help me create the life I want?

ACT Is Not a Religion or a Spiritual Belief System

Many ACT concepts resemble those from various religions, particularly the idea of living life according to your values. But whereas most religions prescribe a ready-made set of values for you, ACT asks you to clarify and connect with your own values. Moreover, ACT does not encourage you to adopt any particular belief system. (Thus, my frequent advice throughout this book: "Don't believe something just because I say so—trust your own experience.") ACT takes the view that if your beliefs work to enrich your life, then that's all that matters.

ACT Is Not Meditation

Many of the exercises in ACT have a meditative feel to them, especially the ones that involve focusing on the breath. But as psychologist Kelly Wilson says, "If you want to learn to meditate, go see a guru."

ACT is not about meditation. There's no special way to sit, no secret mantra, no prayer beads, incense sticks, or candles. ACT is about the practical application of mindfulness skills for the express purpose of making important life changes. And that's it. (Having said that, a daily mindfulness meditation practice can be very helpful in accentuating the skills in this book. If you're interested, read Jon Kabat-Zinn's excellent book, *Wherever You Go, There You Are: Mindfulness Meditation in Everyday Life*.)

ACT Is Not a Pathway to Enlightenment

There are many spiritual or New Age books about reaching enlightenment, all of which place a major emphasis on living in the present moment. ACT stays out of this territory altogether. (ACT is about creating a life, not becoming "enlightened.")

Interestingly, many of these books directly feed into the happiness trap by promising the reader such things as a "pain-free existence, through living fully in the present." While many such books do a fine job of teaching mindfulness concepts, any search for a "pain-free existence" is doomed to failure. The more we try to avoid the basic reality that all human life involves pain, the more we are likely to struggle with that pain when it arises, thereby creating even more suffering. In contrast to such books, ACT aims to help you create a rich, full, and meaningful life while accepting the pain that inevitably comes with living.

So, ACT is not a religious, mystical, or spiritual path, although it may have some parallels. ACT is a scientifically based program for creating a meaningful life through accepting our internal experience, staying present, and acting on our values. And workability is always the deciding factor. So if there's anything in this book (or any other self-help book) that works toward creating the life you want, then please, make use of it. But don't believe anything in this (or any other book) simply because you read it—your own experience trumps someone else's advice.

And that completes this little detour. We're back on the road, and it's time to continue our journey. In the next chapter we'll take a closer look at connection and the many surprising ways it can help you overcome life's obstacles.

20

If You're Breathing, You're Alive

"It's like I'm in a bad dream. I feel like something terrible is going to happen. First I go all dizzy and light-headed, and I can't think straight. Then my heart starts beating like crazy, and I'm sure I'm going to faint or have a heart attack. So I go outside to get some air. But I can't breathe properly. It's like I'm suffocating."

This is Rachel, the secretary you met in chapter 11 (page 88), describing one of her panic attacks. During a panic attack, many people experience symptoms such as a racing heart, tightness in the chest, light-headedness, tingling hands and feet, fears of fainting or dying or going crazy, and a frightening sensation of being unable to breathe.

As we discussed in chapter 11 (page 86), a major part of the problem here is the struggle switch, which creates anxiety about anxiety. But another major part of the problem is rapid, shallow breathing, technically known as "hyperventilation." Whenever we feel stressed, upset, angry, or anxious, our breath rate increases. This is part of the fight-or-flight response, which we covered in chapter 10 (page 84); the increased breath rate gives us increased oxygen in our blood, which helps us prepare either to fight or to run away. But this alters the levels of the gases in our bloodstream, creating a chemical imbalance in the body. And this imbalance triggers a whole series of physical changes in the body, including increased heart rate, increased blood pressure, and increased muscle tension.

And this is why I ask you to practice *slow, deep breathing* with every breathing exercise in this book. By breathing slowly when you're stressed, you will reduce the level of tension in your body. This won't get rid of or control your unpleasant emotions, but it will help you to handle them more effectively. Moreover, your breathing can become a powerful aid—an anchor that steadies you in the midst of emotional storms. So slow, deep breathing is useful for all of us whenever we're stressed in any way. But it's especially important at times when you feel as if you can't breathe properly.

If you're stressed out and your chest is tight and you feel like you can't get enough air, then the problem is probably this: *you're breathing so fast that you're not giving your lungs a chance to empty*! If you don't empty your lungs, then you can't breathe in properly, because you're trying to suck air into a space that's already mostly full. So the first thing you need to do is breathe out—fully and completely exhale, emptying your lungs as much as is physically possible. Once they're empty, you can take a full breath in. And the slower you can take these breaths, the better, because you're helping to rebalance the gases in your bloodstream.

The one thing to be wary of is trying to use your breathing as a control strategy; that is, as a way to get rid of unpleasant emotions or create feelings of relaxation. As with all the other acceptance techniques in this book, relaxation will often arise as a by-product—but don't expect it or strive for it, or you'll fall right back into the whole vicious cycle of control.

The Present Moment

Breathing is wonderful. Not only does it keep you alive, it reminds you that you're alive. How do you feel on a crisp, clear morning when you stop and take a breath of fresh air? How do you feel when you breathe a deep sigh of relief after some stressful event? Your breathing never stops until the day you die, and that makes it a perfect aid to help you stay connected.

In a moment I'm going to ask you to take six slow, deep breaths and empty your lungs as much as possible. Once you've emptied your lungs, don't force the in-breath, otherwise you will overinflate them. (You'll know if this happens, because your chest will feel uncomfortably full.)

After a full out-breath, just breathe in gently, and your lungs will fill comfortably by themselves. (As you breathe in, you should notice your tummy pushing outward.) And as you breathe, connect with the movements of your chest and stomach. Notice what you can feel as they rise and fall. Notice the air flowing in and out. Okay, now put the book down and take six slow, deep breaths.

• • • • •

What did you notice? Probably one of the following:

1. An easing of tension
2. A sense of connecting with your body
3. A feeling of slowing down
4. A sense of "letting go"
5. A quieter mind
6. Dizziness, discomfort, or difficulty because it felt strange or hard to breathe in this manner

Hopefully, you experienced one or more of the first five reactions. If you experienced the last one, don't be concerned. The more you're in the habit of shallow, rapid breathing, the stranger or more difficult this exercise will seem. And if you're an especially rapid breather, it may *at first* give you feelings of dizziness or discomfort. If this is true for you, then it's all the more important for you to practice. If you practice taking ten to twenty deep breaths in this manner, every hour or two throughout the day, then within two weeks it'll feel much more natural and comfortable.

Tuning in to your breathing like this can help you "step out of the rat race" for a few moments, to slow down, let go, and collect yourself. More importantly, it can help you connect with what's happening here and now. To demonstrate this, I'm going to ask you to do the exercise again, but with a twist. (First read the instructions, then do it.)

Take ten slow, deep breaths. For the first five, focus on your chest and abdomen; connect with your breathing. For the next five breaths, expand your focus, so that as well as being aware of your breathing, you're also connecting fully with your environment; that is, while noticing your breathing, also notice what you can see, hear, touch, taste, and smell. Ready? Put the book down and give it a try.

• • • • •

What did you notice? Most people report that they feel far more "present" — more connected with where they are and what they're doing. The idea of this exercise, which I call "Breathing to Connect," is to connect with where you are and what you're doing. Once you've done this, you're in the best psychological space to take effective — that is, life-enhancing — action.

Breathing to Connect doesn't have to be exactly ten breaths. You can shorten or lengthen the exercise as you like. So from now on, start Breathing to Connect throughout the day. Practice it at traffic lights, while waiting in line, before you get out of bed in the morning, during your lunch break, while your computer is booting up, while you're waiting for your husband/wife/children to get ready, etc.

Try longer and shorter versions of the exercise. At traffic lights you might have time for only three or four slow, deep breaths. In a slow-moving grocery line, you may have time for thirty or more. You don't have to keep an exact count.

In particular, start Breathing to Connect whenever you're stressed or whenever you realize you're all caught up in thoughts and feelings. In the midst of a tense situation, even one deep breath can give you precious seconds to collect your wits.

The Power of One Deep Breath

If I am with a client who tells me that he intends to go and kill himself, I naturally feel a surge of anxiety. Now, it won't help my client if I get carried away by my thoughts and feelings. So I immediately take one slow, deep breath, and during those few seconds I make room for my anxiety, allow my thoughts to fade into the background, and focus my attention firmly on my client. And until the crisis is resolved, I keep breathing slowly and deeply, allowing my thoughts and feelings to come and go as

I remain fully connected with what I'm doing. In this way my breathing acts as an anchor. It doesn't get rid of my anxiety, but it stops me from getting carried away. It's like a constant, soothing presence in the background, while my attention is focused on taking effective action.

Remember Donna, whose husband and child died in a car crash? For many months afterward, feelings of sadness would suddenly surge within her, out of the blue. Donna found that even one deep breath could give her a foothold to stop that wave of sadness from sweeping her away. She could then breathe into the sadness, make room for it, and reconnect with her experience here and now. Often this sadness triggered a strong urge to drink alcohol. And here again, even one deep breath made a difference. It gave her a few precious seconds to realize what was happening. Then she could make a conscious choice as to whether or not she would act on that urge.

Remember Michelle, whose life revolved around trying to push away deep feelings of unworthiness? Her boss frequently asked her to do extra work, and she had always stayed late to do it, trying to prove that she was worthy. As therapy progressed, Michelle wanted to break this habit, because she realized it was taking valuable time away from her family. (And also there was no extra pay for all that extra work!) Saying yes to her boss was a hard habit to break. She'd been doing it her entire working life and the thought of saying no brought up all sorts of fears. ("What if he gets angry?" "What if he thinks I'm lazy?") But Michelle was willing to feel that fear in order to take her life in the direction she wanted.

Well, the next time her boss made an urgent request only ten minutes before the close of the day, Michelle felt an immediate urge to say yes. But this time she didn't. Instead she took a long, deep breath. Those few seconds were enough for her to collect her wits and say, "I'm sorry, I can't do that now. I have to go home. I'll deal with it first thing tomorrow morning."

Her boss looked astounded. Michelle's anxiety skyrocketed and her mind started telling her all sorts of horror stories. But she connected with her breathing, made room for her thoughts and feelings, and remained focused on the situation at hand. There was an awkward pause that seemed to last several hours and then, to Michelle's astonishment, her boss just smiled and said, "That'll be fine."

BREATHING TO CONNECT: THE FULL PRACTICE

If you really want to get super-duper, whiz-bang fabulous at connection, put aside ten minutes every day to practice Breathing to Connect.

Sit or lie comfortably with your eyes closed. For the first six minutes connect with your breathing. Notice the gentle rise and fall of your rib cage and follow the air as it flows in and out of your lungs. Let any thoughts and feelings come and go, and each time you notice that your attention has wandered, gently refocus. (You'll need to do this again and again . . . and again.) For the next three minutes expand your awareness, so that you're aware of your body and your feelings as well as your breathing. For the final minute open your eyes and connect with the room around you, as well as with your body, your feelings, and your breathing.

For the first week do this exercise ten minutes a day, then gradually increase the duration by two or three minutes per week, until you can do it for twenty minutes at a time. This is a very powerful mindfulness technique, and regular practice will bring noticeable physical and psychological benefits. (This is another exercise that I have recorded on CD. For details, go to the resources section at the end of this book.)

What Should You Do When You're in a Crisis?

No matter how bad the situation you're in, no matter how much pain you may be suffering, start by taking a few deep breaths. If you're breathing, you know you're alive. And as long as you're alive, there's hope. Taking a few breaths in the midst of a crisis gives you valuable time to get present, to notice what's happening and how you're responding, and to think about what effective action you can take. Sometimes there is no immediate action to take. In this case, being present and accepting what you are feeling is the most effective action.

If you use Breathing to Connect at every opportunity, it will start to become second nature. That's important, because otherwise you'll forget to do it at the times you need it most. Especially aim to practice it whenever you get caught up in your thoughts and feelings. And as with all other acceptance techniques, don't turn this into a control strategy.

The goal is to control your breathing, not your feelings. While Breathing to Connect will often give rise to pleasant feelings such as calmness or peacefulness, you won't always get them, so don't come to expect them or try to force them. When Breathing to Connect, allow yourself to feel whatever you're feeling. Make room for those feelings. You don't have to like them; just let them be.

In the midst of an emotional crisis, it can sometimes be hard to remember these insights and techniques. At the end of the book I've included a list of ACT techniques that can be particularly helpful when we are faced with acute upset, fear, panic, depression, and so forth. (See "Suggestions for Crisis Times" on p. 235.)

What's the Role of the Thinking Self in All This?

So far, we've tended to view the thinking self as a hindrance; as something that disconnects us from life by constantly telling us stories. But the thinking self can also be of tremendous help to us—especially when it helps us to simply . . .

21

Tell It Like It Is

Do any of the following thoughts sound familiar? "I'm not doing it right." "It's useless; I may as well just give up now." "This is a waste of time!" "I'm an idiot!" "Why aren't I practicing what I read in that book?" As you work through this book, your thinking self will undoubtedly give you plenty of tongue-lashings like these. But remember, it's not deliberately trying to upset you; it's just doing the job that it evolved to do.

The observing self, as you know, doesn't make judgments. It's like a camera filming a wildlife documentary. When the lion kills the antelope, the camera doesn't judge it as good or bad; it simply records what happens. The thinking self, on the other hand, loves to judge—that's what it does all day long, day in and day out. Go back a hundred thousand years and this makes good sense. Our ancestors needed to make judgments to stay alive: "Is that dark shape a boulder or a bear?" "Is this fruit safe to eat or poisonous?" "Is that person in the distance friend or foe?" If our ancestors made the wrong judgment, they could end up paying with their lives. So over the course of a hundred thousand years our mind became very good at judging and, as a result, today it never stops. "This shouldn't be happening." "This is bad." "That sucks." "It's not fair!"

Obviously, the ability to judge is vital to our well-being. But as we have already seen, many of the mind's judgments are extremely unhelpful, if we fuse with them. All too often they set us up for a struggle—with ourselves, our feelings, or reality itself. As with any unhelpful thought, the aim in ACT is to let such judgments come and go; rather than buying into them, we can simply acknowledge, "It's a judgment."

In using the thinking self to assist in connection, we need to deliberately put aside judgmental ways of talking and instead use factual descriptions.

Factual Descriptions

What do I mean by "factual descriptions"? Well, here's an example: Julia Roberts is a film actress. Now compare this with a few "judgmental descriptions": Julia Roberts is beautiful; Julia Roberts is a wonderfully talented actress; Julia Roberts gets paid too much. In the very first statement all you have are *facts*: Julia Roberts acts in films and she's female. In the following three statements you have *judgments*: she's beautiful, she's talented, and so forth. None of these are *facts*; they're merely opinions.

When we make negative judgments about our experience, we can easily get into a struggle. But when we describe our experience in terms of facts, it helps us connect with what is actually happening.

Now, you are already doing this to some degree when you use phrases such as, "I'm having the thought that . . ." or "I'm having the feeling of . . ." These words are just factual descriptions of your current experience. You are simply stating what is currently happening: that in this moment you're having a thought or feeling. This allows you to stay connected with what is happening, to be present, open, and self-aware. We can build on this skill by giving a running commentary.

By "running commentary" I mean an ongoing factual description, not a judgmental one, of what is taking place from moment to moment. Doing this can help us stay present, even in the midst of powerful feelings.

Here's how Donna used it with her terrible grief: When a wave of sadness hit her, she would silently say to herself:

I'm having that feeling of sadness again. I can feel it in my chest, like a heavy weight. I don't like it, but I know I can make room for it. Taking a few deep breaths now. Breathing into it . . . that's it . . . making room . . . letting it be. Breathing into it . . .

Sometimes Donna would do this on and off for anywhere from a couple of minutes to the better part of an hour, depending on how powerful her feelings of grief were and how quickly they shifted. This helped her stay present so she could then choose to focus on a valued activity instead of drinking. Sometimes she even added that choice into the commentary: "Now, what do I value doing at this moment? Well, I was just about to cook something healthy for dinner. Is this something I value? Yes, it is. So let's focus on chopping up these potatoes."

Once Donna had chosen a valued activity, she would then connect with it fully, through all of her five senses. For example, she carefully observed the appearance and texture of the potatoes, the sounds of peeling and slicing, the feeling of the knife cutting and chopping, and the movements in her arms, hands, and neck.

Over time, as her grieving process continued, these feelings and urges troubled her less and less. And as she got better at expansion, defusion, and connection, she needed the thinking self less and less to assist her.

Some people find running commentary extremely helpful; others don't. So why not give it a try and see how it works? As always, if it's helpful, make use of it. And if it isn't, don't!

We'll return to connection later in the book, when we use it in taking action. But now it's time to identify . . .

22

The Big Story

What do you most dislike about yourself? I've asked this question of thousands of people, either individually or in groups, and here are some of their most common responses:

- I'm too shy/fearful/anxious/needy/fragile/passive.
- I'm stupid/silly/disorganized.
- I'm fat/ugly/unfit/lazy.
- I'm selfish/critical/arrogant/vain.
- I'm judgmental/angry/greedy/aggressive/obnoxious.
- I'm an underachiever/failure/loser.
- I'm boring/dull/predictable/serious/unmotivated/ignorant.

And those are just a few of the responses. The range is almost infinite. Everyone has their own personal dislikes, but all the answers point to the same basic theme: "I'm not good enough as I am. There is something wrong or lacking in me." It's a message our minds send us again and again.

No matter how hard we try or how much we achieve, our thinking self can always find something to dislike, some way in which we are lacking, deficient, not good enough. And this is hardly surprising when we remember the evolution of the human mind. The "Don't get killed!" device of our ancestors helped them survive by constantly comparing them to other members of the clan, to ensure that they didn't get rejected.

And it constantly drew attention to their weaknesses, so they could improve on them and thereby live longer! The problem is, the thinking self's tendency to point out the ways in which we are *not good enough* eventually leads us to feel as if we are unsuccessful, inadequate, unworthy, unlikable, unlovable, incompetent, or whatever your own version of *not good enough* happens to be. We have a common term for this: "low self-esteem."

Low Self-Esteem

What actually is self-esteem? Basically it is an opinion, an opinion you hold about the sort of person you are. High self-esteem is a positive opinion; low self-esteem is a negative one.

Ultimately, self-esteem is a bunch of thoughts about whether or not you're a "good person." And here's the key thing: self-esteem is not a fact; it's just an opinion. That's right. It's not the truth. It's nothing more than a highly subjective judgment. "Fair enough," you might say, "but isn't it important to have a good opinion of yourself?"

Well, not necessarily. First let's consider what an opinion is: it's a story, nothing more than words. Second, it's a judgment, not a factual description. (Remember, "Julia Roberts is a film actress" is a factual description; "Julia Roberts is a very talented actress" is an opinion/judgment.) So self-esteem is basically a judgment that our thinking self makes about us as a person.

Now, suppose we decide that we want "high" self-esteem. How do we go about getting it? What we tend to do is a whole lot of reasoning, justifying, and negotiating until, maybe, we eventually convince our thinking self to declare that we're a "good person." For example, we may put forward the argument: "I'm doing well at my job, I'm exercising regularly, I'm eating healthily, I help people out—so basically, that means I'm a good person." And if we can really believe that last bit about being a "good person," then we have "high" self-esteem. The problem is, with this approach you constantly have to prove that you're a good person. You constantly have to justify this good opinion. You constantly have to challenge those "not good enough" stories. And all that takes a lot of time and effort. In fact, it's rather like playing a never-ending game of chess.

Imagine a game of chess in which the pieces are your own thoughts and feelings. On one side of the board we have the black pieces: all your "bad" thoughts and feelings. On the other side we have the white pieces: all your "good" thoughts and feelings. And there's an ongoing battle between them: the white pieces attacking the black pieces and vice versa. We spend a huge chunk of our life caught up in this game. But it's a war that will never end because there are an infinite number of pieces on both sides. No matter how many pieces get knocked off, they are always replaced by others.

Now, in trying to raise your self-esteem, you gather as many white pieces together as you can with thoughts like, "My boss just gave me a pay raise," "I'm going to the gym three times a week," and so on. As you advance these white pieces across the board, your self-esteem starts to rise. But here's the problem: there's a whole army of black pieces waiting to counterattack! And the moment you slip up—the moment you stop doing any of those things you're using to justify, "I'm a good person"—those black pieces attack, and your self-esteem dissolves like a sugar cube in the rain.

You stop exercising for a few days, and your mind says, "See? You knew it couldn't last!" You lose your temper with a friend, and it says, "What sort of lousy friend are you?" You make a mistake at work, and you get, "Jeez, what a loser!"

So you try to rally some more white pieces. Perhaps you use positive affirmations, repeating over and over things like, "I am a wonderful human being, full of love, strength, and courage." The problem with this approach is that most people don't really believe what they are saying. It's a bit like saying, "I am Superman," or "I am Wonder Woman." No matter how often you said that to yourself, you wouldn't really believe it, would you?

Another problem is that any positive affirmation you use, regardless of whether it's "true," naturally tends to attract a negative response. (The white pieces always attract the black pieces.) To illustrate this, try the following exercise.

ATTRACTION OF OPPOSITES

In this exercise, read each sentence slowly and try your very hardest to believe it. As you do so, notice what thoughts automatically pop into your head.

- I am a human being.
- I am a worthwhile human being.
- I am a lovable, worthwhile human being.
- I am a competent, lovable, worthwhile, human being.
- I am a perfect, competent, lovable, worthwhile human being.

What happened as you tried to believe those thoughts? For most people, the more positive the thought, the more resistance there is, with thoughts popping up such as, "Yeah, right!" "Who are you kidding?" "Stop talking rubbish!" (A few people do actually manage to fuse with the above affirmations and therefore feel wonderful—for a moment. But that feeling won't last very long. Pretty soon the black pieces will attack again.)

Now, I'd like you to do the same exercise with one more sentence:

I am a useless piece of human garbage.

What happened *that* time? Most people automatically produce a positive thought in their own defense, something like, "Hang on a minute, I'm not that bad!" or "No way, I don't believe that." (And again, a tiny number of people totally fuse with the thought and, as a result, feel lousy.)

The reality is, we can find an infinite number of good and bad stories to tell about ourselves and, as long as we're invested in self-esteem, we're going to waste a lot of time in this chess game, fighting an endless battle against our own limitless supply of negative thoughts.

Let's suppose a black piece appears saying, "How could you be such a bloody idiot?" and you rally the white pieces for help: "Of course you're not an idiot. You just made a mistake. You're human." But another black piece appears saying, "Who are you kidding? Look at how you messed it up last time!" And you counterattack with another white piece: "Yeah, but this time I've learned my lesson." Another black piece says, "You're such an idiot, you'll never get it right!"

The battle's heating up with more and more pieces getting involved. And guess what? While all your attention is on this chess game, it's pretty hard to connect with anything else. You disconnect from life and the world around you, totally lost in the struggle with your own opinions.

Is this really how you want to spend your days? Fighting your own thoughts? Trying to prove to yourself that you're a good person? Continually having to justify or earn your worthiness? Wouldn't you prefer just to step out of the battle?

Letting Go of Self-Esteem

If your self-esteem is low, you feel miserable; but if it's high, you're constantly straining to maintain it. (And there's always the background worry that it might fall again.) So what would life be like if you were to let go of self-esteem altogether; if you completely let go of judging yourself as a person?

Of course, your thinking self would still keep making all the usual judgments, but you would see them for what they are—just words— and let them come and go like passing cars. (And if you wanted to use some defusion techniques to help, you could try thanking your mind or acknowledging, "I'm having the thought that I'm not good enough." Or you could simply name the "not good enough" story.)

How does this seem to you as a concept? Weird? Wonderful? Wacky? Undoubtedly it raises a few questions:

Q: Don't I need high self-esteem in order to create a rich and meaningful life?

A: No, you don't. All you need to do is connect with your values and act accordingly.

Q: Doesn't high self-esteem make that easier to do?

A: Sometimes it does, but all too often it doesn't.

Q: Why not?

A: Because continually trying to maintain that high self-esteem can actually pull you away from what you value. Remember Michelle, working late at the office to improve her sense of worthiness, but missing out on spending time with her family? High self-esteem may give you some pleasant feelings in the short term, but in the long run, trying to maintain it will probably exhaust you. Because of the way the human mind has evolved, the "not good enough" story will always return in one form or another. Do you want to spend the rest of your life battling it? Why bother when you can have a fulfilling life without exerting all that effort?

Q: But don't people with high self-esteem have better lives?

A: This is an incredibly popular myth. And sure, *a few* people with high self-esteem do lead better lives, but if you look into the reputable scientific research on high self-esteem, you'll discover that for many people it creates major problems in their lives. It easily leads to arrogance, righteousness, selfishness, egotism, or a false sense of superiority (which then readily feeds into discrimination and prejudice).

One group that particularly suffers is those for whom high self-esteem is largely dependent upon excelling at work. When they perform well, they feel great, but as soon as their performance drops (as it always will, sooner or later), their self-esteem comes crashing down. This leads them into a vicious cycle, putting increasing pressure on themselves to perform ever better, which leads to high stress, fatigue, and burnout. However, the good news is, to lead a rich, full, and meaningful life doesn't depend on self-esteem in the slightest.

Q: So what are you suggesting as an alternative?

A: Don't try to prove yourself. Don't try to think of yourself as a "good person." Don't try to justify your self-worth. Whatever judgments your thinking self makes of you—whether positive or negative—see them for what they are (just words) and let them go.

And at the same time take action in line with your values. Enhance your life by acting on what is meaningful. And when you slip up and stray off course from those values—which I guarantee you will do over and over again—then don't buy into all those harsh self-judgments. Just thank your mind and let those words come and go. Instead, accept that it has happened and that there's no going back. Then connect with where you are and what you're doing; choose a valued direction and take action.

If you step out of the battle to win self-esteem, then what you are left with is . . .

Self-Acceptance

Self-acceptance means being okay with who you are. Treating yourself kindly. Accepting that you're a human being and therefore imperfect. Allowing yourself to mess up, make mistakes, and learn from them.

Self-acceptance means you refuse to buy into the judgments your mind makes about you, whether they're good judgments or bad ones. Instead of judging yourself, you recognize your strengths and your weaknesses, and you do what you can to be the person you want to be. Your mind will tell you an infinite number of stories about what sort of person you are, but you don't have to believe them. Consider the following example.

Have you ever watched a documentary on Africa? What did you see? Crocodiles, lions, antelopes, gorillas, and giraffes? Tribal dances? Warfare? Nelson Mandela? Colorful marketplaces? Amazing mountains? Beautiful villages in the countryside? Poverty-stricken shantytowns? Starving children? You can learn a lot from watching a documentary, but one thing is for sure: a documentary about Africa is not Africa itself.

A documentary can give you impressions of Africa, some dramatic sights and sounds that represent it. But a documentary can't give you the *real-life experience* of Africa: the taste and smell of the food, the feel of the sunlight on your face, the humidity of the jungle, the dryness of the desert, the feel of an elephant's hide, the pleasure of interacting with the people. No matter how brilliantly filmed that documentary is, even if it's a thousand hours long, it can't come close to the experience of actually being there. Why not? Because a documentary about Africa is not the same thing as Africa itself.

Similarly, a documentary about you would not be the same thing as you yourself. Even if that documentary lasted for a thousand hours and included all sorts of relevant scenes from your life, all sorts of interviews with people who know you, and all sorts of fascinating details about your innermost secrets, even then the documentary would not be you.

To really clarify this, think of the person you love most on this planet. Now, which would you prefer to spend time with, the actual living person or a documentary about that person? So, there's this huge difference between who we are and any documentary that anyone could ever make about us, no matter how "truthful" that documentary may be. And I've put "truthful" in quotation marks because all documentaries are hopelessly biased in that they only show you a tiny part of the big picture. Since the advent of cheap video, the typical hour-long television documentary is the "best" of literally dozens, if not hundreds of hours of footage. So inevitably it's going to be quite biased.

And the bias of a human film director is nothing compared to the bias of our thinking self. Out of an entire lifetime of experience, literally hundreds of thousands of hours of archival "film footage," our thinking self selects a few dramatic memories, edits them together with some related judgments and opinions, and turns them into a powerful documentary entitled *This Is Who I Am* (and it usually has a subtitle: *Why I'm Not Good Enough*). And the problem is, when we watch that documentary, we forget that it's just a heavily edited video. Instead, we believe that we are that video! But in the same way that a documentary of Africa is not Africa, a documentary of you is not you.

Your self-image, your self-esteem, your judgments about the sort of person you are, all these things are nothing more than thoughts, images, and memories. They are *not* you. Like it or not, the simple fact is . . .

23

You're Not Who You Think You Are

Have you ever heard these sayings? "I think, therefore I am." "Learn to think for yourself." "Develop your mind." "Think positively." "Think harder." Our society teaches us that thinking is the ultimate human ability. Lateral thinking, rational thinking, logical thinking, positive thinking, optimistic thinking: all are widely encouraged. And, of course, thinking skills are very important in life. Indeed, part 3 of this book places a major emphasis on effective thinking. But there's more to you than your thoughts.

No matter what you're thinking, imagining, or remembering, there's a part of you that's separate from your thoughts; a part of you that's able to observe your mind in action, to notice what it's doing. In this book, I've called it the observing self, and you've already been using it as you worked through various exercises. Whenever you observe your breath or your thoughts or your feelings, the observing self is the part of you that's doing all the observing.

We can talk about "self" in many different ways, but in everyday communication, we commonly refer to only two aspects of self: the physical self (our body) and the thinking self (our mind). The observing self is so rarely talked about, we don't even have a word for it in our language. This is a pity, because it is very important; without it we have no capacity for self-awareness or psychological flexibility. So let's take the time to learn a bit more about it.

The following exercise consists of a series of short instructions. Make sure you actually *do* them, instead of just reading them, otherwise you won't get the benefits. (And where it says "ten seconds" or "thirty seconds" don't actually count them or you'll interfere with the exercise; just use that figure as a rough guide.)

NOTICE YOURSELF NOTICING

1. For ten seconds, close your eyes and just notice all the sounds you can hear.
2. Now do that again but this time, *as* you notice what you can hear, *be aware* that you're noticing.
3. Now for ten seconds, look around and notice what you can see.
4. Now do that again but this time, *as* you notice what you can see, *be aware* that you're noticing.
5. For ten seconds, notice the position of your body: where your feet are, what's supporting you, how curved your spine is.
6. Now do that again but this time, *as* you notice your body, *be aware* that you're noticing.
7. For ten seconds, close your eyes and notice what you're thinking.
8. Now do that again but this time, *as* you notice your thoughts, *be aware* that you're noticing.
9. Now sniff the air and notice what you can smell. (If you can't smell anything, just notice the sensations inside your nostrils.)
10. Now do that again, and *as* you do it, *be aware* that you're noticing.
11. Notice what you can taste in your mouth. (If you can't taste anything, just notice the sensations inside your mouth.)
12. Now do that again, and this time, *as* you do it, *be aware* that you're noticing.
13. Now for the second time, close your eyes and notice what you're thinking (for about ten seconds).
14. Now do that again, but this time, *as* you notice your thoughts, *be aware* that you're noticing them.
15. Now for ten seconds, slowly wiggle your fingers and notice their movements.
16. Now do that again, and *as* you do it, *be aware* that you're noticing.

17. Now scan your body and focus in on any feeling or sensation that grabs your attention and for ten seconds, really observe it.
18. Now observe that feeling again, but this time, *as you do so, be aware* that you're observing it.
19. Now take three slow, deep breaths and really notice your breathing.
20. Now do that again, and *as you do so, be aware* that you're noticing.
21. Now for the third time, close your eyes (for ten seconds) and notice what you're thinking.
22. Now do that again but this time, *as you notice your thoughts, be aware* that you're noticing them.

In that exercise hopefully you found that part of you that is aware of everything you see, hear, touch, taste, smell, feel, think, and do. (If you didn't, please go back and do the exercise again.) This part of you is what ACT calls "the observing self."

The Observing Self

The observing self is not a thought or a feeling. Rather, it's a viewpoint from which you can observe thoughts and feelings. In some ways, a better term for it is "pure awareness" because that's all it is: awareness.

Whatever you are thinking, whatever you are feeling, whatever you're sensing, whatever you're doing, this part of you is always there, aware of it. You know what you're thinking or feeling only because this part of you is aware of your thoughts and feelings. Without this observing self, you have no capacity for self-awareness.

Now consider this: Your thoughts and images change continuously. (How many have passed through your head in the past hour?) Sometimes they're pleasant, sometimes painful, sometimes helpful, sometimes a hindrance. But one thing's for sure: they keep changing. The same is true for your feelings and sensations. Sometimes you feel sad, sometimes you feel happy. Sometimes calm, sometimes angry. Sometimes healthy, sometimes sick. (How many different sensations and feelings have you experienced in the past hour?)

Your body also changes continuously. The body you have now is not the one you had as a baby, as a child, or as a teenager. You generate a whole new set of skin every six weeks. A whole new liver every three months. And every single year, 95 percent of the atoms in your body are replaced by new ones.

Your roles also change continuously throughout life. Sometimes you are in the role of parent, child, brother, sister, aunt, or uncle. At other times you take roles such as client, customer, patient, helper, assistant, employer, employee, contractor, citizen, friend, enemy, student, teacher, adviser, mentor, visitor, tourist, and so on. Just notice the role you're in right now: that of a reader.

So the roles you play and your thoughts, images, feelings, sensations, and physical body all change continuously throughout your life. But the observing self does not change. The observing self is a viewpoint from which to observe everything else—thoughts, feelings, sensations, roles, body, etc. But the viewpoint itself never changes.

You can think of it as the part of you that truly "sees the big picture." By "big picture" I mean everything you ever experience, everything you ever see, hear, touch, taste, smell, think, feel, or do. The observing self "sees" it all.

Qualities of the Observing Self

The observing self can't be judged as good or bad, right or wrong, because all it does is observe. If you do "the wrong thing" or a "bad thing," the observing self is not in any way responsible; it merely notices what you've done and helps make you aware of it (thereby enabling you to learn from it). Moreover, the observing self will never judge you because judgments are thoughts and the observing self cannot think. It notices thoughts, but it cannot generate them.

The observing self sees things as they are, without judging, criticizing, or doing any of the other thinking processes that set us up for a struggle with reality. Therefore, it gives acceptance in its truest, purest form.

The observing self can't be improved on in any way. It is always there, working perfectly and seamlessly. All you need do is access it.

The observing self can't be harmed, either. If your body is physically damaged through illness, aging, or injury, the observing self notices that damage. And if pain arises, the observing self notices that pain. And if bad thoughts or memories happen as a result, the observing self notices those, too. But neither the physical damage nor the painful feelings nor any of the bad thoughts or memories can harm that part of you that observes them.

In summary:

- The observing self is there from birth to death and is unchanging.
- It observes everything you do but never judges you.
- It cannot be hurt or damaged in any way.
- It is always there, even if we forget about it or know nothing of it.
- It is the source of true acceptance.
- It is not a "thing." It is not made of physical matter, and has no physical properties. You cannot measure it or quantify it or extract it or examine it. You can only know it through direct experience.
- It cannot be improved on in any way; therefore, it is perfect.

When you look at the summary above, you can see some parallels between ACT and various religions or spiritual traditions. But ACT places no religious beliefs on this observing self. You are free to conceptualize it as you wish and call it what you will.

You can think of the observing self as being like the sky, while thoughts and feelings are like the weather—constantly changing. And no matter how bad the weather, no matter how violent the thunderstorm, no matter how turbulent the wind, rain, and hail, the sky always has room for it and cannot be hurt or harmed by it in any way. Even hurricanes and tsunamis, which may wreak havoc upon the land, are unable to hurt or harm the sky. And, of course, as time passes, the weather will change, while, out beyond the weather patterns, the sky remains as pure and clear as ever.

The Observing Self in Everyday Life

In normal, everyday life, all we get are "glimpses" of the observing self because most of the time it's obscured by a constant flow of thoughts.

Again, this is like the sky, which may at times be completely obscured by clouds. But even when we can't see the sky, we know it's there, and if we rise up high enough above those clouds, we will *always* find it.

Similarly, when we rise above our thoughts, we "find" the observing self: a viewpoint from which we can observe our negative self-judgments or self-limiting beliefs without being hurt by them. From the perspective of the observing self, you can look at that "documentary" about who you are and see it for what it is: a collection of words and pictures compiled by the thinking self. The thinking self tells you that the documentary is you. But all you need to do is step back and observe it, and in that moment, it's clear you are not the documentary.

This often raises the question, "If I'm not my mind, then who am I?" Well, there's a whole book in that one question, but the shortest, simplest answer is this: "you" are a combination of the thinking self, the physical self, and the observing self. They are all just different aspects of "you." However, the observing self is the only aspect of you that never changes; it is there in the same form from the day you are born to the day you die.

Accessing your observing self is very simple to do. Choose anything that you are aware of—a sight, sound, smell, taste, sensation, thought, feeling, movement, body part, material object—literally anything. Focus your attention on whatever you have chosen, and *as* you're noticing it, *be aware* you're noticing. That's it. That's all you need to do. So let's do it right now. First read the instructions, then give it a try.

WHERE ARE YOUR THOUGHTS?

Close your eyes and take thirty seconds to observe your thoughts. Notice where they seem to be located in space—are they above you, in front of you, inside you—and notice, are they more like pictures, words, or sounds? (If your thoughts all disappear, then just notice the empty space.) And as you notice those thoughts (or empty space), be aware that you're noticing them. Notice, there are your thoughts—and there you are observing them. Now read the instructions once more, then close your eyes and and give it a try.

• • • • •

Next take thirty seconds to observe your breathing. And as you notice the breath coming and going, be aware that you're noticing it. Notice, there is your breath—and there you are observing it. Now read the instructions once more, then close your eyes and give it a try.

• • • • •

Finally take thirty seconds to observe your body, scanning it from head to toe. And as you notice your body, be aware that you're noticing it. Notice, there is your body—and there you are observing it. Now read the instructions once more, then close your eyes and give it a try.

• • • • •

So, that's all there is to it. Of course, it's very hard to stay in the "psychological space" of the observing self. Almost instantly, your thinking self will start analyzing or commenting on what's happening, and as you get caught up in those thoughts, the observing self seems to disappear. But this is just an illusion. The observing self is always there and instantly accessible whenever you want it. Because of the nature of the mind, you will get caught up in its stories again and again and again, until the day you die. However, the moment you realize this is happening, you can instantly "step back," observe the story, and free yourself from its clutches.

The End?

This brings us to the end of part 2, and hopefully your psychological flexibility is already increasing. You may recall, psychological flexibility has two major components: (1) the ability to adapt to a situation with openness, awareness, and focus, *and* (2) the ability to take effective action, guided by values. In part 2, we've focused mainly on the first of these components: bringing openness, awareness, and focus (i.e., mindfulness) to whatever is happening in this moment. In part 3, we will mainly focus on the second component: clarifying values and taking effective action. Inevitably, as you start taking action to create the life you want, you will face many fears and encounter many unpleasant thoughts and feelings. But more and more, using defusion, expansion, and connection, you can learn to overcome such obstacles. And isn't it good to know that the observing self is always there to help you? It's like a safe haven inside you; a place from where you can observe even the most difficult thoughts, feelings, and memories, knowing they can never harm the "you" who observes them.

PART THREE

Creating a Life Worth Living

24

Follow Your Heart

What's it all about? What are you here for? What makes your life worth living? It's amazing how many of us have never deeply considered these questions. We go through life following the same routine, day after day. But in order to create a rich, full, and meaningful life, we need to stop to reflect on what we're doing and why we're doing it. So it's time now to ask yourself:

- Deep down inside, what is important to you?
- What do you want your life to be about?
- What sort of person do you want to be?
- What sort of relationships do you want to build?
- If you weren't struggling with your feelings or avoiding your fears, what would you channel your time and energy into doing?

Don't worry if you don't have all these answers on the tip of your tongue. Over the next few chapters we'll explore them in depth, and your answers will connect you with . . .

Your Values

We've already touched on values several times in this book. Values are:

- Our heart's deepest desires: how we want to be, what we want to stand for, and how we want to relate to the world around us.

- Leading principles that can guide us and motivate us as we move through life.

When you go through life guided by your values, not only do you gain a sense of vitality and joyfulness, but you also experience that life can be rich, full, and meaningful, even when bad things happen. Take the case of my good friend Fred.

Fred had a business venture that went horribly wrong. As a result, he and his wife lost almost everything they owned, including their house. In dire financial straits, they decided to move from the city out to the country, so they could live in a nice place with affordable rent. There Fred found a job at a local boarding school that catered to foreign students, mainly teenagers from China and Korea.

This job was totally unrelated to Fred's business experience. His duties involved maintaining order and security in the boardinghouse, ensuring that the kids did their homework, and making sure they went to bed at the right time. He also slept in the boardinghouse overnight and prepared the children for school the next morning.

Many people in Fred's shoes would have been deeply depressed. After all, he'd lost his business, his house, and a huge amount of money, and now he was stuck in a low-paying job that kept him away from his wife five nights a week!

But Fred realized he had two choices: he could dwell on his losses, beat himself up, and make himself miserable—or he could make the most of it. Fortunately, he chose the latter.

Fred had always valued coaching, mentoring, and supporting others, and now he decided to bring these values into the workplace. So he began to teach the children useful skills, such as how to iron their clothes and cook simple meals. He also organized the school's first-ever talent contest and helped the kids film a humorous documentary about student life. On top of this, he became the students' unofficial counselor. Many of them came to him for help and advice in dealing with their various troubles: relationship difficulties, family issues, problems with studies, and so on. None of these things were part of Fred's job description, and he didn't get any extra pay for doing them; he did them purely and simply because he valued giving and caring. And as a result, what could have been a mundane job became work that was meaningful and satisfying.

At the same time, Fred didn't give up on his career. While he needed this job in the short term to pay the bills, he continued to look for work that he genuinely desired. He'd always been an excellent organizer and administrator with a particular interest in theatrical and musical events, and this was the area he most wanted to work in. Eventually, after many months of applying for all sorts of work, Fred found a job as the organizer of a local arts festival. It was a job that fulfilled him, paid him well, and allowed him to spend a lot more time with his wife.

Fred's story serves as a great example of how we can live by our values even when life gets tough. It's also a good example of how we can find fulfillment in any job, even one we don't want, by bringing our values into the workplace. That way, even while we search or train for a better job, we can find satisfaction within the one we have.

Values Versus Goals

It's important to recognize that values are not the same as goals. A value is a direction we desire to keep moving in, an ongoing process that never reaches an end. For example, the desire to be a loving and caring partner is a value. It's ongoing for the rest of your life. The moment you stop being loving and caring, you are no longer living by that value.

A goal is a desired outcome that can be achieved or completed. For example, the desire to get married is a goal. Once achieved, it's done and can be crossed off the list. Once you're married, you're married, whether you're loving and kind, or hard-hearted and uncaring.

So a value is like heading west. No matter how far you travel, there's always farther west you can go. Whereas a goal is like the mountain or river you wish to cross on your journey. Once you've gone over it, it's a "done deal."

If you want a better job, that's a goal. Once you've gotten it, the goal is achieved. But if you want to apply yourself fully at work, to be attentive to detail, supportive to your colleagues, friendly to customers, and engaged in what you're doing, those are values.

Why Are Values
So Important?

Auschwitz was the most notorious of the Nazi death camps. We can scarcely begin to imagine what took place there: the horrific abuse and torture, the extremes of human degradation, and the countless deaths through disease, violence, starvation, and the infamous gas chambers. Viktor Frankl was a Jewish psychiatrist who survived years of unspeakable horror in Auschwitz and other camps, which he described in gruesome detail in his awe-inspiring book *Man's Search for Meaning*.

One of the most fascinating revelations in this book is that, contrary to what you would expect, the people who survived longest in the death camps were often not the physically fittest and strongest, but rather, those who were most connected with a purpose in life. If prisoners could connect with something they valued, such as a loving relationship with their children or an important book they wished to write, that connection gave them something to live for, something that made it worthwhile to endure all that suffering. Those who could not connect with a deeper value soon lost the will to live.

Frankl's own sense of purpose came from several sources. For example, he deeply valued his loving relationship with his wife and was determined to survive so he could one day see her again. Many a time during strenuous work shifts in the snow, with his feet in agony from frostbite and his body racked with pain from brutal beatings, he would conjure up a mental image of his wife and think about how much he loved her. That sense of love was enough to keep him going.

Another of Frankl's values lay in helping others, and so, throughout his time in the camps, he consistently helped other prisoners to cope with their suffering. He listened compassionately to their woes, gave them words of kindness and inspiration, and tended to the sick and the dying. Most importantly, he helped people to connect with their own deepest values so they could find a sense of meaning, of purpose. This would then quite literally give them the strength to survive. As the great philosopher Friedrich Nietzsche once said, "He who has a why to live for, can bear almost any how."

Values Make Life
Worth Living

Life involves hard work. All meaningful projects require effort, whether you're raising kids, renovating your house, learning kung fu, or starting your own business. These things are challenging. Unfortunately, all too often, when faced with a challenge, we think, "It's too hard," and we give up or avoid it. That's where our values come in.

Connecting with our values gives us a sense that our hard work is worth the effort. For instance, if we value connecting with nature, this makes it worth the effort to organize a trip to the countryside. If we value being a loving parent, it's worth taking the time to play with our kids. If we value our health, we're willing to exercise on a regular basis despite the inconvenience. In this way, values act as motivators. We may not feel like exercising, but valuing our health can give us the will to "just do it."

The same principle applies to life in general. Many of my clients ask questions such as, "What's the point of life?" "Is this all there is?" "Why don't I feel excited about anything?" Others say things such as, "Maybe the world would be better off without me." "I have nothing to offer." "Sometimes I wish I could go to bed and never wake up again."

Such thoughts are commonplace not just among the 10 percent of adults who suffer from depression at any given time, but also among the rest of the population. Values provide a powerful antidote, a way to give your life purpose, meaning, and passion.

IMAGINE YOU'RE EIGHTY YEARS OLD

Here's a simple exercise to get you started on clarifying your values. Please take a few minutes to write out or think about your answers. (Hint: you'll get more out of it if you write your answers down.)

Imagine that you're eighty years old and you're looking back on your life as it is today. Then finish the following sentences:

- I spent too much time worrying about . . .
- I spent too little time doing things such as . . .

- If I could go back in time, then what I would do differently from today onward is . . .

• • • • •

How did it go? For many people this simple exercise is quite an eye-opener. It often points to a big difference between what we *value* doing and what we are *actually* doing. In the next chapter we'll explore your values in more detail. In the meantime, I'll leave you with this oft-quoted extract from *Man's Search for Meaning*:

We who lived in concentration camps can remember the men who walked through the huts comforting others, giving away their last piece of bread. They may have been few in number, but they offer sufficient proof that everything can be taken from a man but one thing: the last of human freedoms—to choose one's attitude in any given set of circumstances, to choose one's own way.

25

The Big Question

Deep down inside, what do you *really* want? Often when I ask people this question, they say things such as:

- "I just want to be happy."
- "I want to be rich."
- "I want to be successful."
- "I want respect."
- "I want a great job."
- "I just want to get married and have kids."

Now, these may all be truthful answers, but they're not particularly "deep," reflective, or carefully considered. So in this chapter we will go deeper, to connect with your heart and soul, to really consider, *deep down inside*, what is important to you. What do you want to stand for in life? What sort of personal qualities do you want to cultivate? How do you want to be toward others?

Remember, values are your heart's deepest desires for how you want to behave in life, the way you want to interact with and relate to the world, other people, and yourself. Values describe *what* you want to do, and *how* you want to do it—how you want to behave toward your friends, your family, your neighbors, your body, your environment, your work, etc.

The exercise that follows is adapted from the work of psychologists Kelly Wilson and Tobias Lundgren. We will focus on four important domains of life: (1) relationships, (2) work/education, (3) leisure, and (4) personal growth/health. Please keep in mind that not everyone has the same values, and this is not a test to see whether you have the "right" ones. There is no right or wrong, no good or bad, when it comes to values. What you value is what you value—end of story! Also, please answer as if there were no obstacles in your way; nothing to stop you from acting the way you truly want to.

You may find some values that overlap—e.g., if playing sports is important to you, that might come under both Leisure and Personal Growth/ Health. You may recall, values are not the same as goals. Values are about *ongoing action*—what you want to keep doing for the rest of your life; whereas goals can be completed or crossed off a list. For example, if you want to take your kids on vacation, that's a goal—once achieved, it can be crossed off the list as "task accomplished," "over and done." However, if you want to be loving, caring, and supportive toward your kids, that is a value: it involves ongoing action forever. (We'll look at setting goals later, once you know what your values are.)

Finally, it's preferable that you actually *write down* your answers. Writing concentrates your mind and helps you to remember your answers. If, however, you're not willing to write, then at least *think long and hard* about your answers. (You can download a free worksheet from the resources page on www.thehappinesstrap.com.)

As you work through this questionnaire, it's important to keep in mind that feelings are not values. If you write, "I want to feel confident," or "I want to feel happy," those are not values. Values are about what you want to *do*, not about how you want to *feel*. You need to ask yourself, "If I *did* feel this way—if I did feel happy or relaxed or confident or secure or loved or respected or admired, then what would I *do* differently? How would I *act* differently? How would I *behave* differently toward others and toward myself? What would I *do* more of or less of?" Your answers will then reveal your underlying values.

The Life Values Questionnaire

1. Relationships

This includes relationships with your partner, children, parents, relatives, friends, neighbors, fellow students or athletes, and all your other social contacts.

- What sort of relationships do you want to build?
- How do you want to behave in these relationships?
- What personal qualities do you want to develop?
- How would you treat others if you were the "ideal you" in those relationships?
- What sort of ongoing activities do you want to do with some of these people?

Notice that these questions are *all about you*, about how *you* would like to be and what *you* would like to contribute to these relationships. Why? Because the only aspect of a relationship you have control over is the way you behave. You have no control over how the other person thinks, feels or behaves. Sure, you can *influence* them, but you can't *control* them. And what's the best way to influence them? With your actions: the things you do with your arms and your legs and your mouth! And of course, those actions will be most effective when they're aligned with your values. For instance, in any relationship you can request changes from the other person and set boundaries on what you will and won't accept. And obviously, this will be far more effective if you say these things while behaving as the "ideal you," rather than shouting, yelling, crying, threatening, or being manipulative. This basic principle applies to all the relationships you have with friends, family, colleagues, and employees— and anyone else you'll ever meet! Remember the golden rule: treat others as you'd like them to treat you.

Sometimes, as a response to the above questions, people describe what sort of friends they want or what sort of partner they want—but then they are describing goals, not values. To get to your values, you need to ask, "If I did have the sort of partner or friends that I want, *how would I behave* toward them? What personal qualities would *I* like to bring to this relationship?" Of course it can be useful to think about the sort of partner or friends you'd ideally like—then you can set yourself a goal to go out and find them. But in the meantime, you can make the most of whatever relationships you're in right now by bringing your own values into play. And if the other person in any given relationship is abusive or hostile or treating you badly in some way, then you will need to consider your values around assertiveness, self-respect, self-protection, and taking care of yourself. In some cases, you may even need to terminate the relationship.

2. Work/Education

This refers to your workplace and career, education and knowledge, or further skills development. (This may also include volunteering and other forms of unpaid work.)

- What personal qualities would you like to bring to the workplace (or place of study)?
- How would you behave toward your colleagues/employees/customers/clients/fellow students, if you were the "ideal you"?
- What sort of relationships do you want to build in the workplace or at school?
- What skills, knowledge, or personal qualities do you want to develop?

Sometimes people write descriptions of the ideal jobs, careers, or courses they want, but then they are describing goals, not values. To get to your values around work or education, you need to ask, "If I did have the job, career, or course that I really want, how would I behave differently when I'm doing it? What personal qualities would I like to bring to that enterprise?" Naturally, if you don't like your current job or course, it makes sense to start retraining or looking around for a more meaningful or satisfying job (or course). In the meantime, you can make the most of whatever job or course you're in by bringing your values into play there. (Remember Fred, in the last chapter?)

3. Personal Growth/Health

This refers to activities that enhance your ongoing development as a human being physically, emotionally, and mentally. This may include religious or spiritual activities, psychotherapy, addiction recovery, meditation, yoga, getting out into nature, exercise, nutrition, volunteer work, creativity, joining political or environmental causes, and addressing health risks like smoking.

- What ongoing activities would you like to start or take up again?
- What groups or centers would you like to join?
- What lifestyle changes would you like to make?

4. Leisure

This refers to how you play, relax, stimulate, or enjoy yourself; your hobbies, sports, artistic pursuits, or other activities for rest, recreation, fun, mental stimulation, and creativity.

- What sorts of hobbies, sports, or leisure activities do you want to participate in?
- On an ongoing basis, how do you wish to relax, unwind, or have fun, in healthy, life-enhancing ways?
- What sorts of activities would you like to take up or do more of?

The Bull's-Eye

Okay, so if you've written about your values (or at least, thought long and hard about them), then it's time to fill in the "bull's-eye," a tool developed by Swedish psychologist Tobias Lundgren. First, read through (or remember) your answers above. Then make an X in each area of the dart board on the next page, to represent where you stand today. An X in the bull's-eye (the center of the board) means that you are living fully by your values in that area of life. An X far from bull's-eye means that you are way off the mark in terms of living by your values. Since there are four areas of valued living, you should mark four Xs on the dart board. (You can also download a free copy of this diagram from the resources page on www.thehappinesstrap.com.)

THE BULL'S EYE

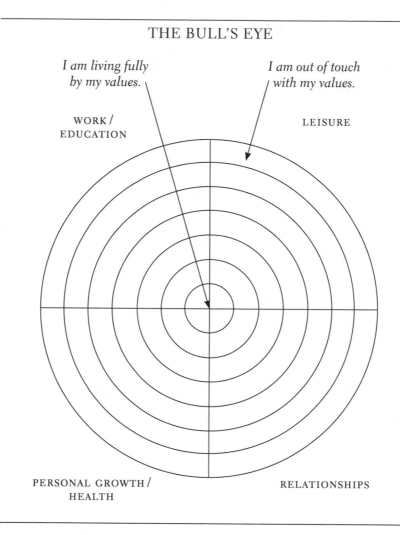

I am living fully by my values.

I am out of touch with my values.

WORK / EDUCATION

LEISURE

PERSONAL GROWTH / HEALTH

RELATIONSHIPS

So what does this exercise tell you about what is important in your life, and what you are currently neglecting, avoiding, or missing out on? Did you have trouble completing it, because it brought up uncomfortable thoughts and feelings? Often when we connect with our values, we realize that we've been neglecting them for a long time, and this can be very painful. But this is not an excuse to beat yourself up! The fact is, all of us lose touch with our values at times and act out in self-defeating ways. Dwelling on that is pointless, because there's nothing we can do to change the past. What's important is to connect with our values *here and now* and to use them to guide and motivate our actions *from this point onward*. (So if your mind does start beating up on you, simply thank it.)

You may have found that you skipped parts of this exercise or avoided answering the questions because you fused with unhelpful thoughts like, "It's too hard," "I can't be bothered," "I don't know if these are my real values," or "I'm just setting myself up for disappointment." If this is the case, read through the next chapter on troubleshooting. Once you've done that, come back and work through this chapter again. If, on the other hand, you've completed this chapter to your satisfaction, then you can skip the next one and go straight to chapter 27 (page 183).

Time to Reflect

Now it's time to look back over your answers and reflect on them. Ask yourself:

- Which of the above values are the most important to me?
- Which of them am I actively living by right now?
- Which of them am I most neglecting?
- Which are the most important to start working on right away?

Write your answers down and hold on to them. You'll need them for the next few chapters.

Our lives revolve around relationships—with other people, with ourselves, with our bodies, with our work, with our environment. The more you act in line with your values, the better will be the quality of those relationships and therefore the more enjoyable and rewarding your life will be.

In the next few chapters we're going to look at how you can use your values to set purposeful goals, create meaning, and find fulfillment. In the meantime, reflect further on this chapter. Discuss your values with friends or loved ones. Write about those values in more detail. And look for opportunities to act on them in daily life.

26

Troubleshooting Values

The demons are getting restless. They know what you're up to: you're plotting a new course, planning to steer that boat toward land. Below I've listed a few that might try to stop you.

The "I Don't Know If These Are My Real Values" Demon

This is a very sneaky demon. It seeks to undermine your confidence by having you doubt your answers. The way to deal with it is to answer these questions:

1. If a miracle could happen so that you automatically had the full approval of everyone who matters to you (and therefore you weren't trying to please or impress anyone), then what sort of things would you do with your life and what sort of person would you try to be?
2. If you weren't guided by other people's judgments and opinions, what would you do differently in your life?

The questions above are to help you clarify what you really want, so that you are living by your own values and not someone else's. The next three questions ask you to think about your death, as a way of clarifying what's important in life.

1. If you could somehow listen in on your own funeral and the people you most care about were there, what sort of things would

you love to hear them say about you? What would you like them to think about the role you played in their lives?

2. If you knew you had only one year left to live, how would you like to be as a person and what would you like to do during that time?

3. If you were trapped in a collapsed building and knew you had only a few minutes to live, who would you call on your cell phone and what would you say to them? What does your answer reveal about what's important to you?

The "I Don't Know What I Want" Demon

If you're not sure what you want, ask yourself this: If I could have any values I wanted, which ones would I choose?

Whatever values you would choose, those already are your values! Why? Because the fact that you would choose them shows you already value them!

The "I Don't Want to Think about It" Demon

If you've experienced a lot of failure, frustration, or disappointment in your life, then you may be afraid to acknowledge what you really want for fear it will only lead to more of the same. If so, remind yourself that the past is the past—it's over and can't be changed. But no matter what has happened in the past, you can make changes right now that will allow you to create a new future. So do the exercises, and if uncomfortable feelings arise, breathe into them, make room for them, and keep focused on the questions.

The "I'm Just Setting Myself Up for Disappointment" Demon

This sneaky critter is usually accompanied by several of its buddies, such as, "I'll only fail if I try" or "I don't deserve anything better in life" or "I can't change." Remember, these are nothing more than "pop-up" thoughts. So thank your mind, let them come and go and refocus on answering the questions.

The "I Can't Be Bothered Right Now; I'll Do It Later" Demon

You know this creature far too well to believe what it says. You know that "later" never gets here. So thank your mind and answer the questions now.

The "But My Values Conflict with Each Other" Demon

This demon is making a valid point: at times your values will pull you in different directions. But don't let that stop you from acting on them. It just means you'll need to find a compromise. Sometimes you'll need to focus more on one value than another. For example, a few years ago my older brother was working at a high-powered job that required him to spend a lot of time traveling away from home. There was a major conflict of values here. On the one hand he valued being a loving father, and he wanted to spend as much time with his young son as possible. On the other hand, he valued his work and, of course, the financial benefits it gave to his family. These conflicting values are common for many parents, and there's rarely a perfect solution. The important thing is to find the best balance that you can. So when my brother was away on overseas trips, he called home every night to read his son a bedtime story over the phone. Sure, it wasn't the same as being there in person, but it was nonetheless a very loving act.

The reality is, there will be times that you have to focus more on some domains of life than others. This calls for soul-searching, for asking yourself, "What's most important at this moment in my life, given all my conflicting concerns?" Then choose to act on that value, rather than wasting your time uselessly worrying about what you might be giving up or missing out on.

There are many other demons that will try to deter you—but you already know that they're only a bunch of words. So let them be and focus your attention where it's most useful: on plotting the course, steering the ship onward, and thoroughly appreciating the voyage. Therefore, if you didn't complete the exercises in the last chapter, then go back and do them now. And if you have completed them, it's time to take the next step of . . .

27

The Thousand-Mile Journey

So you've identified your values, and you know what really matters to you, deep inside. Now what?

Well, now it's time to take action. A rich, full, and meaningful life doesn't spontaneously happen just because you've identified your values. It happens through taking action, guided by those values. So take a few moments to reflect once more on what's important to you. As you read down the list below, mentally remind yourself of your values in each domain:

1. Family
2. Marriage and other intimate relationships
3. Friendships
4. Employment
5. Education and personal development
6. Recreation, fun, and leisure
7. Spirituality
8. Community life
9. Environment and nature
10. Health and body

Now ask yourself, "In which of these domains am I most out of touch with my values?" If several (or all) domains come to mind, consider, "Which domain is the most important to start working on right now?"

It's important to start with only one domain at a time, because if you try to make too many changes at once, you'll probably just feel overwhelmed and quit. (Naturally, over time, the idea is to work on all the important areas of your life. However, frequently as you start making changes in one domain, it spills over into others, a sort of domino effect.) So once you've identified which domain to begin with, it's time to start setting meaningful goals.

Setting Meaningful Goals

Sorry to be a nag, but once again, I have to stress the importance of writing down your answers to these exercises. Research shows that you're far likelier to take action if you write your goals down than if you just think about them. So please, for the sake of a better life, put down this book and go get a pen and paper!

There are five steps in setting meaningful goals.

Step 1: Summarize Your Values

Write a brief description of the domain and the values you're going to work on. For example, "In the domain of family, I value being open, honest, loving, and supportive."

Step 2: Set an Immediate Goal

Ask yourself, "What's the smallest, easiest thing I can do today that is consistent with this value?" It's always good to boost your confidence by starting with a small, easy goal—one that can be accomplished right away. For example, if your value is to be a loving partner, your goal may be, "During my lunch break, I'll call my wife and tell her I love her."

When setting goals, it's important to be specific about what you will do. For instance, "I'll go swimming for thirty minutes, twice a week," as opposed to making vague statements like "I'll do more exercise." Also, specify when and where you'll do it. For example, "I'll go for a run in the park right after work on Wednesday."

Starting with small, easy goals will help you defeat the "it's all too hard" demon, which is guaranteed to raise its ugly head right about now. And it's always useful to remind yourself of this ancient Chinese proverb by the great philosopher Lao Tzu: "A journey of a thousand miles begins with one step."

Step 3: Set Some Short-Term Goals

Ask yourself, "What small things can I do over the next few days and weeks that are consistent with this value?" Remember: be specific. What actions will you take? When and where will you do them? For example, in the domain of work, if you value helping others but your current job gives you little opportunity to do so, then one of your short-term goals might be: "Each night this week, between nine and ten, I will do some research on the Internet to find a more meaningful job" or "Tomorrow morning I will make an appointment with a career counselor."

Step 4: Set Some Medium-Range Goals

Ask yourself, "What larger challenges can I set for the next few weeks and months that will take me in my valued direction?" Again, be specific. For example, if your value is about looking after your health, a medium-range goal might be: "Three nights a week, I will cook dinner using recipes from a healthy cookbook," or "I will go for a twenty-minute walk every morning."

Step 5: Set Some Long-Term Goals

Ask yourself, "What major challenges can I set for the next few years, which will take me in my valued direction?" This is where you dare to think big. What would you like to achieve in the next few years? Where would you like to be five years from now? Long-term goals may include anything from changing careers and having kids to sailing around the world. Allow yourself to dream.

Don't Set a Dead Person's Goal

Never set as your goal something that a dead person can do better than you. For example, to stop eating chocolate—that's something a dead person can do better than you because, no matter what, they'll definitely never, ever eat chocolate again. Or to stop feeling depressed— that's something a dead person can do better than you, because they'll never feel depressed again. Any goal that is about *not* doing something or *stopping* doing something is a dead person's goal. To convert it to a live person's goal (i.e., something that a live person can do better than a dead one) you need to ask yourself, "If I was no longer doing this activity (or feeling this way or thinking like this), what *would* I be doing with my time? How would I be acting differently?" For example, suppose you answered, "If I was no longer smoking, I'd be going for a walk after lunch and breathing in the fresh air instead of puffing on a cigarette." Okay, so make that your goal. After lunch, instead of having a cigarette, get up and go for a walk and breathe in the fresh air. That is definitely something you can do better than a dead person.

Imagine Yourself Taking Effective Action

In much of this book we've looked at the dark side of the mind: the problems that happen when we fuse with unhelpful thoughts or images. But fusion can also be very useful, in the right context. For example, in the world of elite sports, top athletes use a technique called "visualization" as a way of enhancing their performance. They vividly imagine themselves performing at their peak. They "see" themselves in their mind's eye alert, focused, using their skills to the very best of their ability, and this process of mental rehearsal actually improves their performance in reality.

And yes, you guessed it, it's now time for you to do the same thing. Once you've set a goal, close your eyes and spend a few moments vividly imagining yourself taking effective action. (Imagine this in any way that comes naturally. Some people can easily conjure up vivid mental pictures, but others imagine more with words, sounds, or feelings.) See yourself, feel yourself, and hear yourself taking effective action to achieve your goal. Notice what you're saying and what you're doing. Keep rehearsing, until it's clear to you what your actions are. (And if your mind starts trying to disrupt this process with stories like "I can't do it" or "It's too hard," then simply say, "Thanks, Mind!" and continue the exercise.)

Most books on visualization or mental rehearsal will encourage you to imagine yourself feeling relaxed and confident as you take action. I strongly advise against this because those are feelings over which you have very little control, and if your goal is particularly challenging, it's very unlikely that you will feel relaxed and confident. You're far more likely to have feelings of anxiety and self-doubt. So I suggest that in your mental rehearsals, focus on what is most in your control: your actions. Imagine yourself taking action to the very best of your ability, saying and doing the things that are most likely to be effective. And also imagine yourself making room for whatever thoughts and feelings show up in the moment and continuing to take effective action, no matter how you feel.

It's helpful to practice this exercise again and again, whenever you set yourself challenging new goals. Of course, it won't guarantee that you'll achieve your goals, but it'll make it more likely. So put the book down now, close your eyes, and spend a few minutes imagining yourself taking effective action.

●　●　●　●　●

Some Examples of Goal-Setting

Remember Soula? She had just turned thirty-three and was feeling sad and lonely because she was still single while all her friends were in long-term relationships. In the domain of intimate relationships, Soula valued being loving, caring, open, sensual, and fun-loving. But because she didn't currently have a partner, her major long-term goal was to find one. Therefore, her short-term goals included research into dating agencies and social clubs and asking her friends to fix her up with blind dates. More challenging, medium-term goals included *actually joining* a dating agency and *actually going out* on some blind dates.

Remember Donna, who lost her husband and child in a tragic car accident? Once she had given up drinking alcohol, she was faced with rebuilding her life, piece by piece. She had lost a lot of weight and her body was in terrible condition, so she began by focusing on the domain of physical health. Small, easy, short-term goals included buying a healthy sandwich at lunchtime and going to bed at a reasonable hour. More challenging medium-range goals included signing up for a yoga class and hiking in the countryside on weekends.

And how about Michelle, the woman who worked late out of fear of angering her boss? Once she identified that she wished to spend more quality time with her family, she started saying no to extra work and made sure she left the office at a reasonable hour. Her values were to be a loving, caring mother, to be present and connected with her children, and to spend more quality time with them, engaging in shared activities rather than simply waiting on them hand and foot. Small goals included listening intently to her kids when they talked to her (instead of being caught up in her own thoughts) and putting aside an hour two nights a week to play a family game, such as *Scrabble* or *Monopoly*. Larger, mid-range goals included organizing a family picnic or outing most weekends. A long-term goal was to take the children to Spain.

Action Plans

Once you've identified your goals, you need to break them down into an action plan. Ask yourself:

- What smaller steps are required in order to complete this goal?
- What resources (if any) do I need in order to take these steps?
- When, specifically, will I carry out these actions?

For example, if you value exercising and your goal is to go to the gym three times a week, your action plan may include (a) joining the gym, (b) getting your gym wear together, (c) planning the times you will go, and (d) rearranging your schedule to accommodate this activity. The resources you may need are (a) money to join the gym, (b) your gym gear (sneakers, shorts, T-shirt, towel, and a bag to carry it in). Next, specify when you will actually do this. For example, "I'll pack my bag tonight.

Then I'll join the gym tomorrow after work, and I'll start my first session then and there."

If you find you're lacking the necessary resources to achieve your goal, you have two options:

1. Change your goal. For example, if you don't have the money for a gym membership, go for a run instead.
2. Make a plan of action to obtain the necessary resources. For example, borrow the money.

Sometimes the resource you need is actually a skill. For example, if your goal is to improve your relationship, you may need to learn some communication or assertiveness skills. If your goal is to improve your finances, you may need to learn some investment skills. If this is the case, make a plan as to how you will learn this skill. What books can you read or courses can you take?

Now, take a pen and paper (or a laptop) and do these exercises. Even if you don't have time to complete it right now, at least get your feet wet, even for five or ten minutes. It's amazing, once you get started, how much can happen in a short time. Write down:

1. Your values
2. Your goals (immediate, short-term, mid-range, and long-term)
3. Your action plan for those goals

This may seem like a lot of hard work right now, but the more you practice thinking this way—moving from values to goals to specific actions—the more it will start to come naturally, without the need for all this planning.

Does This Sound a Bit Contrived?

Values? Goals? Action plans? Does this all sound just a little too contrived. Too orderly, too detailed, too structured? What happened to good old spontaneity, to taking life as it comes?

Well, unfortunately, these things are the nuts and bolts that give our lives structure and help them function well. There's plenty of room for spontaneity once your boat is sailing in the right direction, but first you've got to choose where you're heading, then use a map and compass to plot your course. And, of course, you mustn't forget to appreciate the voyage.

Change happens in an instant. The moment you steer that ship toward shore, you are successfully creating a meaningful life. Your mind will try to tell you that the most important thing is to reach the shore, but that's not really the case. The most important thing is *sailing toward shore*. When you're drifting aimlessly at sea, you feel half dead. But when you're heading for shore, you feel alive. As renowned author and educator Helen Keller put it: "Life is either a daring adventure or nothing."

Of course, that shore you're heading for may be a long way off, and it may take weeks or months or even years to get there. And sometimes when you get there, you may not even like it. So it's sensible to make the most out of the voyage. Look around, take it in, and notice what you can see, hear, smell, touch, and taste. When we move in a valued direction, every moment of our journey becomes meaningful. So engage fully in everything you do along the way. Practice your mindfulness skills: be open to and interested in your experience. That way, you'll find it stimulating, satisfying, and invigorating, even during those times when the going gets tough. And you may be surprised at the many opportunities you discover for . . .

28

Finding Fulfillment

In Western society we tend to lead a goal-focused life. Life is all about achievement, and success is usually defined in terms of status, wealth, and power. Typically, we aren't that closely connected with our values, and because of that, we can easily get caught up in goals that are not truly meaningful to us. For instance, we can get so caught up in earning money or furthering our careers that we neglect to spend time with our family—the classic workaholic syndrome.

A more destructive version of the goal-focused life is when our goals center on avoiding painful thoughts and feelings. As we've already seen, this leads to major suffering in the form of addictions, self-defeating behaviors, and increasing remoteness from what we really want.

That's why in ACT we advocate a values-focused life. Yes, we set goals, because goals are essential to a fulfilling, rewarding life—but we set them guided by our values. This means the goals we pursue are a lot more personally meaningful. And life itself becomes much more rewarding. We live more in the present and we appreciate what we have. So even as we move toward our goals, we find a deep satisfaction in life as it is right now.

Think of it this way. There are two kids in the back of a car, and Mom's taking them to Disneyland, which is a three-hour drive away. One kid has only one aim: to get to Disneyland as fast as possible. He's sitting on the edge of his seat, in a state of constant frustration. Every few minutes he's whining, "Are we there yet?" "I'm bored." "How much longer?" The second kid, however, has two aims: to get to Disneyland as fast as possible *and* to appreciate the journey. So this kid is looking out the window, noticing all the fields full of cows and sheep, watching in fascination at the giant trucks zooming past, waving out of the window at friendly pedestrians. He's not frustrated. He's living in the moment, appreciating where he is, rather than focusing on where he's not.

Now if the car breaks down halfway and the kids never reach Disneyland, then which child has had the most rewarding journey? And if they do make it to Disneyland, obviously both kids will have a great reward—but still, only one of them has enjoyed the journey.

The values-focused life will always be more fulfilling than the goal-focused life because you get to appreciate the journey even as you're moving toward your goals. What's more, in a values-focused life, you're likelier to achieve your goals. Why? Because if you make sure that your goals are in line with your values, then you'll be more motivated to pursue them.

Abundance

Connecting with your values and acting on them gives you a sense of contentment, fulfillment, and abundance because living by your values gives you satisfaction *right now*. For instance, suppose you really want to buy a house. Buying a house is a goal (it can be achieved and crossed off the list). But suppose it will be a long time before you can actually buy that house. If you believe you can't lead a rich and full life until you've achieved that goal, then you will be pretty miserable.

So ask yourself, "What's this goal in the service of? What will it enable me to do that's truly meaningful?" If the answer is, "To provide security for my family," then you've identified a core value: taking good care of your family. And taking care of your family is something you can do right now, in a hundred and one different ways. For example, you can cook a healthy dinner, read a story to your kids, or give your partner a hug.

This doesn't mean you give up on your goals. If you want to buy a house, start saving! But you don't have to wait until you buy that house to have the satisfaction of caring for your family.

Let's take another example. Suppose you have the long-term goal of being a doctor. The training will take some time, and I'd hate for you to spend ten years of your life doggedly focused on that goal, thinking you can't be fulfilled until you've achieved it. So ask yourself, "What is this goal in the service of? What will it enable me to do that's truly meaningful?"

Suppose you answer, "I'd be able to help people." Now you've identified a core value: helping others. And helping others is something you can do right now. You can visit an elderly relative, contribute money to a worthy cause, help a fellow student with their homework, or even do some volunteer work.

This doesn't mean you give up your goal of becoming a doctor. What it means is, for the next ten years, while you're working toward that goal, you have the ongoing satisfaction of living by your values — in this case, helping people.

"But suppose my motivation isn't helping people," you may be saying. "Suppose I just want to get rich." Well, for starters, being rich is a goal, not a value. It's a goal because it can be achieved and crossed off the list. But to answer this question more fully, here's a transcript of a session I had with Jeff. Jeff was a businessman in his mid-thirties, making a good living but obsessed with earning more. He was making himself miserable by constantly focusing on all the people he knew who were richer than he was. I asked Jeff, "What do you really want?"

Jeff: To be absolutely honest, I want to be stinking rich.

Russ: Fair enough. If you were stinking rich, what would that enable you to do?

Jeff: Lots of things.

Russ: Such as?

Jeff: Travel around the world.

Russ: What would you do on your travels?

Jeff: I'd laze around on beaches, explore exotic countries, visit the wonders of the world.

Russ: Okay. What do you value about lazing around on beaches?

Jeff: It's relaxing. It's a great way to chill out.

Russ: And what do you value about visiting exotic countries?

Jeff: Meeting new people, tasting new cuisines, discovering exotic arts and crafts.

Russ: Okay. Now, I want to be clear on this. I'm not for a moment suggesting that you give up on your goal. If you want to be rich, by all means, go for it. In fact, if you want, we can spend some time brainstorming how to make that happen. But I'd hate to see you spend the next ten years feeling miserable because you think you have to be rich before you can find fulfillment. See, you identified "relaxing" and "chilling out" as activities you value. Well, there's a zillion different ways you can relax and chill out right now, and you don't have to be rich. You could have a hot bath, listen to some music, do yoga . . .

Jeff: Yeah, but I really *do* like lazing on beaches.

Russ: Absolutely. And so it makes sense to save up your money and plan a beach holiday. But you don't have to wait until you're rich to have the satisfaction of relaxing—that's something you can do every day. And it's the same for those other values. For example, if you value tasting exotic cuisine, how could you do that right now?

Jeff: I guess I could try some ethnic restaurants.

Russ: Yeah, or some ethnic cookbooks.

Jeff: Yes, but that's not the same as eating the local food in a foreign country.

Russ: I'm not suggesting that it is. I'm just pointing out that if you truly value eating exotic food, you don't have to wait until you're rich enough to travel the world. And the same goes for discovering little-known arts and crafts. If you wanted to do that right now, what could you do?

Jeff: Go to art galleries?

Russ: Exactly. Or visit museums or local arts-and-crafts fairs. Or you could read about it or research it on the Internet.

Jeff: Yeah, but that's not the same as—

Russ: I know. And again, if you want to travel overseas, then it makes sense to save money and plan for it. All I'm saying is, if you value relaxing, eating different foods, and learning about unusual arts and crafts, you can do all these things right now. You don't have to go through life desperately wanting. Now, let's come back to your goal of being rich. Why else is that important?

Jeff: Because people look up to you when you're rich.

Russ: Well, I don't know if that's always the case, but let's assume you're right. What's so important about having people look up to you?

Jeff: They treat you better. They respect you.

Russ: So let's suppose that people treated you well and respected you and looked up to you. What would that enable you to do?

Jeff: I guess I'd be more at ease. I wouldn't have to try and impress anyone. I could just be myself.

Russ: So what you really value is being yourself? Being genuine?

Jeff: Yeah. I just want to be me.

Russ: Okay. So can you be genuine right now? Do you have to wait until you're rich?

Jeff: It's easier if you're rich.

Russ: Maybe so. But are you going to wait until you're rich before you give yourself the satisfaction of being genuine?

Jeff: What if I'm genuine and people don't like me?

Russ: Do you want to spend your life building friendships with people who only like you because you're rich?

Jeff: No.

Russ: What sort of friendships do you want to build?

Jeff: Ones where I can be myself; where I can be accepted for who I am.

Russ: Okay. So if you value being genuine, why not start right now in the relationships you already have? Ask yourself, "What's one small thing I could say or do that would be truer to the real me?"

As you can see, Jeff was quite convinced that he needed to be rich before he could find satisfaction in life. But over time, as Jeff chose increasingly to live by his values, he found a deep sense of fulfillment—even as he pursued his financial and business goals.

Riches, Fame, and Success

Jeff's case is hardly unique. Many people want to be rich, famous, and successful. Yet these things are goals, not values. To get to the values underlying a goal, you need to ask yourself, "What's this goal in the service of? What will it enable me to do that's truly meaningful?"

As in Jeff's case, you may need to ask this question several times over to get to the underlying value. There may be many motivating factors underlying the desire for fame, wealth, and success. One particularly common motivation is to have others look up to you, admire you, respect you. And why is this important? Because, as Jeff put it, then you wouldn't have to try to impress anyone. You'd have much less fear of rejection. And that would then allow you to "be yourself."

Most of us go through life too scared to let others see who we really are. We're ruled by the thought: "They won't like me if they know what I'm really like." The cost of this is enormous: we end up disconnected from the people around us, and our relationships lack intimacy, depth, and openness. We end up going through life wearing a mask, trying to hide who we are—putting on a show in order to win approval, love, or friendship. Why does this happen? Simple: because we've fused with the "I'm not good enough" story. Our minds tell us we have to be rich or famous or successful to compensate for our shortcomings; that only then will we be accepted, liked, and loved. And, foolishly, we believe them!

So if being genuine and open is what you value, why wait until you're rich, famous, or successful? Why not start being more yourself today? Let people start to know you. Be real. Be authentic. Be open. Ask yourself, "What's one small thing I could say or do that would be more consistent with the real me?"

As with acting on any value, always start with small, short-term goals. For example, in a conversation or group discussion, you might express your genuine opinion rather than an insincere one designed to win approval. Or you might share a bit more about what's really happening in your life, instead of pretending that everything's perfectly all right.

(Of course, you'll have to defuse the "they won't like me/respect me/approve of me" stories.)

Other Motivations

Needless to say, there are plenty of other motivations for becoming rich, famous, or successful. But if you work through them as I did with Jeff, you'll eventually get down to core values—which you can live by right now. For example, you might say, "If I were rich, I could buy a helicopter and learn to fly it." The values underlying this may be about learning new skills, personal development, having fun, or facing your fears. All these are values you can live by right here and now without being rich or owning a helicopter.

Let's return to Soula, whose major goal was to find a loving partner. You'll recall that she set herself some smaller goals, including joining a dating agency and going on some blind dates. These were important steps, to be sure. But as long as Soula believed that life could not be fulfilling without a partner, she was setting herself up for a lot of unnecessary suffering. So I asked her to connect with the values underlying that goal. As a partner, Soula valued being loving, caring, open, sensual, and fun. I pointed out to her that although she didn't have a partner right now, she could still act on those values in other domains of her life.

"But that's not the same as having a partner," she said.

"Absolutely right," I replied. "But which helps you to lead a fuller life: living by your values here and now or making yourself miserable by constantly focusing on a goal you haven't achieved yet?"

Soula got the point. She started to be more loving and caring toward her family and more open and fun-loving with her friends and coworkers. She also chose to be more sensual with herself—having regular massages, taking soothing hot baths, and enjoying erotic literature. And the result? Life became far more satisfying, even though she hadn't yet achieved her major goal.

What If You Do Achieve That Goal?

The truth is, no matter how many goals you achieve, there will always be something else you want. You know what it's like. You get that fabulous new job and it's all very exciting, but how long before the novelty wears off? How long before you're yearning for something new? Or you get that pay raise and you love having all that extra money, but how long before you take it for granted and want more? Or perhaps you meet the partner of your dreams and fall madly in love, but how long before you start noticing that your dream lover snores or wears the same socks three days in a row?

If you're living a goal-focused life, then no matter what you have, it's never enough. Not so with the values-focused life, because your values are always available to you, no matter what your circumstance. (Remember Viktor Frankl, who lived by his values while stuck in a Nazi concentration camp.)

So if you're feeling miserable because you haven't yet achieved a particular goal, here's what to do. First find the values underlying your goal and then ask yourself, "What's a small action I can take right now that's consistent with those values?" Next go ahead and take action (and do it mindfully).

Your values are always with you, always available. And being faithful to them is usually deeply rewarding. So the more you embrace your values, the greater your sense of fulfillment. In the next chapter we'll learn how this can give us . . .

29

A Life of Plenty

Have you ever gazed in wonder at a brilliant sunset or an impossibly large full moon or the ocean waves crashing against a rocky shore? Ever looked adoringly into the eyes of your child or your partner? Reveled in the aroma of baking pies or the fragrant scent of jasmine or roses? Listened in delight to a singing bird or a purring cat or the laughter of a small child?

So far in this book, we've spent a lot of time on handling unpleasant thoughts and feelings, but precious little on enhancing the positive ones. This is deliberate. Our whole society, and the self-help movement in particular, is so focused on creating positive feelings that this focus itself has become a major component of the happiness trap. The more your life is focused on having pleasant feelings, the more you'll struggle against the uncomfortable ones, creating and intensifying the whole vicious cycle of struggle and suffering.

But as a beneficial by-product of creating a meaningful life, all sorts of positive experiences and emotions will happen. So it only makes sense to appreciate these things to the fullest while avoiding the trap of making them your main goal in life. Every day is a wealth of opportunities to appreciate the world we live in. Practicing your mindfulness skills will help you make the most of your life right now, even as you take action to change it for the better. We have always had expressions like, "Count your blessings" and "Stop and smell the roses." These sayings point to the abundance in our lives. We are surrounded by wonderful things, but sadly, we usually take them for granted. So here are a few suggestions for waking up and experiencing the richness of the world around you:

- When you eat something, take the opportunity to savor it, to fully taste it. Let your thoughts come and go and focus on the sensations in your mouth. Most of the time when we eat and drink, we're scarcely aware of what we're doing. Given that eating is a pleasurable activity, why not take the time to appreciate it fully? Instead of wolfing your food down, eat it slowly—actually chew it. (After all, you wouldn't watch a video on fast forward, so why eat your food that way?)
- Next time it's raining, pay attention to the sound of it: the rhythm, the pitch, the ebb and flow of the volume. And notice the intricate patterns of the raindrops on the windows. And when it stops, go for a walk and notice the freshness of the air and the way the sidewalks glisten as if they'd been polished.
- Next time it's sunny, take a few moments to appreciate the warmth and the light. Notice how everything brightens: houses, flowers, trees, the sky, people. Go for a walk, listen to the birds, and notice how the sun feels against your skin.
- When you hug or kiss someone—or even shake hands—fully engage in it. Notice what you can feel. Let your warmth and openness flow through that contact.
- Next time you're feeling happy or calm or joyful or content or some other pleasant emotion, take the opportunity to fully notice what that feels like. Notice what you feel in your body. Notice how you're breathing, talking, or gesturing. Notice any urges, thoughts, memories, sensations, and images. Take a few moments to really drink in this emotion, to marvel that you are capable of having such experiences. (But don't try to hold on to it.)
- Look with new eyes at the people you care about, as if you'd never seen them before. Do this with your spouse or partner, friends, family, children, coworkers, colleagues. Notice how they walk, talk, eat and drink, and gesture with their faces, bodies, and hands. Notice their facial expressions. Notice the lines on their faces and the color of their eyes.

- Before you get out of bed in the morning, take ten deep breaths and focus on the movement of your lungs. Cultivate a sense of wonder that you are alive, that your lungs have provided you with oxygen all night long, even while you were fast asleep.

When you act with openness, kindness, and acceptance, the chances are, you'll receive the same in return. (And if you don't, you may have to make some choices about what sort of people you spend your time with.) So as your relationships improve, make the most of them. Savor those positive interactions. Make sure you're present. Catch yourself drifting off into the land of thoughts and bring your attention back to whomever you're with.

A great job, a loving partner, a home of your own: all these are goals. As you work toward them, connect with the values underlying them. Notice that you're living by those values and appreciate the satisfaction this brings.

When you achieve goals that are in line with your values, there's often a pleasant emotion of some sort. Notice how it feels and enjoy it. Even tiny, easy goals can give great satisfaction when achieved. For example, I feel enormous satisfaction when I tidy my desktop, cook a healthy dinner, or send a brief e-mail to an overseas relative. So appreciate and savor those feelings. It's all too easy to miss them when the thinking self tries to distract you with "not good enough" stories.

It's All about Connection

As you open your eyes and notice the things you've previously taken for granted, you'll notice more opportunities, you'll be more stimulated and interested, you'll find more contentment, and your relationships will improve. I like to put it like this: *Life gives most to those who make the most of what life gives.*

And now, after all that focus on positive emotion, it's time for another reminder: don't get too attached to pleasant feelings. Don't center your life on chasing them. Pleasant feelings will come and go, just like every other feeling. So enjoy them and appreciate them when they visit, but don't cling to them! Just let them come and go as they please.

At times mindfulness is easy and at times it's incredibly hard. In fact, one of the hardest things about mindfulness is remembering to practice it. Steven Hayes likens it to riding a bicycle. When you're on a bike, you're always about to fall over; you're always catching yourself, continually adjusting your balance. So it is with mindfulness. No matter how deeply connected we are with our here-and-now experience, our thoughts will continually pull us out of it. We have to keep catching ourselves, realizing our mind has pulled us off balance yet again. (And remember how hard it was to balance when you first started learning to ride that bike? And how it got easier over time?)

Life is like climbing a mountain: there are easy stretches and tough ones. But if you're open and interested in your experience, then the obstacles you encounter will help you to learn, grow, and develop, so that as time goes on, your climbing skills improve. Naturally, it's far easier to be mindful when the going is easy, than when it gets tough. Yet the more you face your difficulties with mindfulness, the more you'll find you grow stronger, calmer, and wiser. This is easier said than done, but you can do it. Especially once you know the secret of . . .

30

Facing FEAR

How's it all going? Are you taking action? Making some meaningful changes in your life? If not, you've probably come up against at least one of the four major obstacles to change. These obstacles are so universal, they even form their own acronym—FEAR:

Fusion
Excessive expectations
Avoidance of discomfort
Remoteness from values

Let's take a look at these obstacles one by one.

Fusion

As soon as you start setting goals, Radio Doom and Gloom will start to broadcast, "I can't do it," "It's too hard," "I'm wasting my time," "There's no point in trying," and a whole playlist of other golden oldies. If you fuse with these thoughts, you're in trouble.

The solution is to use your defusion skills: see these thoughts for what they are (just words), let them come and go, and return your focus to taking effective action.

Excessive Expectations

Your expectations may be excessive in several ways:

1. Your goals are too big. You expect to do too much, too soon.

2. You expect to achieve goals for which you lack the necessary skills or resources.
3. You expect to do it all perfectly, to make no mistakes.

If your goals are too big, you'll feel overwhelmed and will probably give up. The solution is to break your goals down into smaller chunks. Ask yourself, "What's the smallest, easiest step I could take that would bring me a little closer to achieving this goal?" Then go ahead and do it.

And once you've taken that step, ask the question again: "What's the next small, easy step that would bring me a little bit closer to my goal?" (It's like that old joke: How do you eat an elephant? One mouthful at a time!) And obviously, if your time frame is unrealistic, then you'll need to extend it.

Similarly, if you lack the skills to achieve your goals, then you will need to take the necessary time to learn them. You can't expect to cycle the Tour de France if you haven't first learned to ride a bike. And if you lack the resources you need to achieve your goal (such as time, money, health, energy, support, equipment, or knowledge), then you will need to figure out how you can find them. If there is no way to find these resources in your current situation, then you will need to let go of that goal for now and set yourself a more realistic one.

As for making mistakes, that's a fundamental part of being human. Almost every activity you take for granted today—reading, talking, walking, riding a bicycle—was once hard to do. (Think how many times a baby falls on its bottom while learning to walk.) But the point is, you learned by making mistakes. You learned what not to do and you learned how to do it differently, so you became more effective. Making mistakes is an essential part of learning, so embrace it. Let go of aiming for perfection. It's much more satisfying and fulfilling to be human.

Avoidance of Discomfort

The more you try to avoid discomfort, the harder it will be to make important changes. Change involves risk. It requires facing your fears and stepping out of your comfort zone—both of which point to one thing: change will usually give rise to uncomfortable feelings.

By now you're well aware of the whole vicious cycle that results when we try to avoid discomfort. The only effective solution is true acceptance (not tolerance or "putting up with it"). Therefore, practice your expansion skills, make room for your discomfort, and focus on taking effective action.

Of course, setting and working toward goals will not only create discomfort. It will often generate pleasant feelings, too, such as excitement and curiosity and the pleasure and satisfaction you'll feel when you finally achieve those goals. But discomfort often comes first!

Remoteness from Your Values

It's not enough to clarify your values—you need to connect with them on a regular basis. You need to know what's important in your heart and to remind yourself often. And you need to make sure your goals are in line with those values. Doing this will provide you with motivation, inspiration, and meaning.

But if you're remote from your values, it's all too easy to lose heart, give up, or get sidetracked. The more remote you are from your deepest values, the more your goals seem pointless, meaningless, or insignificant. Obviously, this doesn't do much for motivation.

The solution? Connect with your values. If you haven't already done so, write them down. Read them through and change them as required. Share them with someone you trust. Reread them on a regular basis. First thing in the morning, mentally go over them. At the end of each week, take a few minutes to check in with yourself and ask: "How true have I been to my values?"

Back to Fusion

So that's FEAR: fusion, expectations, avoidance, and remoteness. And of these four obstacles, fusion is probably the most common. When we fuse with unhelpful thoughts, the demons on our boat grow bigger and nastier. And the scariest of all these demons is called, "You will fail!" which usually hangs around with several of its pals, "There's no point in trying," "You're wasting your time," and "Look at all the times you failed in the past."

If we take these demons seriously and give them our full attention, our boat is doomed to drifting out at sea. So when they appear, it's helpful to remember this quote by Henry James: "Until you try, you don't know what you can't do." In setting goals for ourselves, we're talking about what is possible, not what is certain. There's very little certainty in this world. You can't even be certain that you'll still be alive tomorrow. So none of us can ever be certain that we'll achieve our goals. But what we can be certain of is this: if we don't even attempt to achieve them, there's no possibility of success.

Of course, your mind will not be swayed by this logic for long. The "give up" story will appear again and again. Therefore, again and again, you will need to detect and defuse it.

Your mind will also tell you lots of "what if?" stories. "What if I try and I fail?" "What if I invest all that time and energy and money and it all amounts to nothing?" "What if I make a fool of myself?" If you let yourself get hooked in by these stories, you can easily waste endless hours debating with yourself instead of taking action. So acknowledge the stories, thank your mind, let the stories come and go, then choose actions that are aligned with your values. Make your choices based on what you truly care about instead of on keeping the demons below deck. And especially be alert for a type of unhelpful thinking known as reason-giving.

Reason-Giving

The mind is very good at coming up with reasons for not doing the things we really want to do. Take physical exercise. In most Western countries, over 40 percent of the adult population is overweight or obese, and in the United States alone it's over 50 percent. Yet almost all of us, deep down inside, value our health. Sure, many of us neglect our health (some of us much of the time), but that doesn't mean we don't value it. It just means we're not taking action. To clarify this, ask yourself, "Which would I prefer: a healthy body or an unhealthy one?"

The fact is, most of us would prefer to eat healthier and exercise more. So why don't we? Well, part of the explanation is that our mind is a genius at giving us reasons not to: "I don't have enough time," "I'm too tired," "I can't be bothered," "It's too cold."

The first thing to realize is that reasons are just thoughts. The second thing is that thoughts do not control your behavior. Does that sound surprising to you? Well, check your own experience. How often have you had the thought, "I can't do this!" and then gone ahead and done it? How often have you thought, "Yes, I am going to do this!" and then not followed through on it? How often have you thought about taking hurtful, harmful, hostile, or self-defeating actions but not actually done so? (It's just as well that thoughts don't control our behavior; otherwise most of us would be in prison, laid up in the hospital, or dead.)

To demonstrate conclusively that thoughts do not control your behavior, do these two exercises:

1. Think to yourself, "I can't scratch my head! I can't scratch my head!" and as you do, lift your arm and scratch your head.
2. Think to yourself, "I have to close this book! I have to close this book!" and as you do, keep the book open.

How'd you do? No doubt you found that you could still take those actions even though your mind said you couldn't. What this shows you is that while your thoughts can *influence* your actions, they don't actually *control* your actions. When do thoughts have the *most* influence over your actions? When you *fuse* with them. When do thoughts have *least* influence? When you *defuse* them.

This means that reasons are not a problem unless we fuse with them: take them as the literal truth or treat them as commands we must obey. Therefore, it's important to realize that reasons are not facts.

Here's an example of a reason: "I can't go for a run because I'm too tired." But does being tired make you physically unable to run? Of course not. You can feel tired and still go for a run. (In fact, ask any athlete — they'll tell you that sometimes they can feel tired or sluggish and end up having one of their best workouts.)

Here's an example of a fact: "I can't go for a run because a spinal injury has completely paralyzed my legs." Does spinal paralysis of the legs make it physically impossible to run? Yes. So the above statement is a fact.

Reasons are basically just excuses, things we say to justify what we do (or don't do). Can you feel as though you don't have enough time but still exercise? Can you feel tired but still exercise? Can you notice that it's cold outside but still exercise? Obviously, the answer to all these questions is yes.

As soon as you have to face any sort of challenge, your mind will come up with a whole list of reasons not to do it: "I'm too tired," "It's too hard," "I'll only fail," "It's too expensive," "It'll take too long," "I'm too depressed," etc. And that's okay, as long as we see these reasons for what they are: just excuses.

How Do You Tell an Excuse from a Fact?

Often we know full well when we're making excuses—we just need to be honest with ourselves. But if you've set a valued goal and your mind gives you a reason not to attempt it, sometimes it's not so clear that this is just an excuse. So if you're genuinely unsure whether the thought is merely an excuse for inaction or a statement of fact about something that truly is impossible, just ask yourself this question: "If the person you care about more than anyone else in the world were kidnapped, and the kidnappers told you they will never release that person until you start taking some valued action, would you do it?" If the answer is yes, then you know that any reason (for not taking that action) is merely an excuse.

"Ah, yes," you may be saying, "but that's just a silly hypothetical question. In the real world, the person I love has not been kidnapped."

Right you are. But what's at stake in the real world is something equally important: your life! Do you want to live a life in which you do the things that are really meaningful to you? Or do you want to live a life of drifting aimlessly, letting your demons run the ship?

"Okay," I hear you say. "I agree that I could attempt this goal, but it's not that important to me."

The question here is, are you being honest with yourself or are you just buying into another thought? If the goal you're avoiding is truly unimportant to you, fine, don't attempt it. But make sure you check in with your values. And if this goal really is something you value, then you are faced with a choice: either act in accordance with what you value or let yourself be pushed around by your own thoughts.

In particular, you need to watch out for this sneaky thought: "If this were really so important to me, I'd be doing it already!" This thought is just another "reason" in disguise. The reasoning goes something like this: "I haven't taken action up to now, which means it can't really be that important, which means it's not a true value of mine, which means there's no point in putting any effort into it."

This reasoning is based on the false assumption that humans will naturally act in line with their values. But if this were true, there'd be no need for a therapy such as ACT. The fact is, many of us don't act on our values for long periods of time: months, years, or even decades. But those values are always there deep inside us, no matter how remote from them we are. A value is like your body: even if you've totally neglected it for years, it's still there, it's still an essential part of your life, and it's never too late to connect with it.

You may say, "But it's not that easy. These reasons seem so convincing."

That's right. They do seem convincing if you fuse with them. So you need to remember, they're just thoughts. You can then defuse them in a number of different ways:

- You can simply notice them and label them. Each time a reason pops into your head, acknowledge it by silently saying, "Reason-giving."
- You can say to yourself, "Thanks, Mind!"
- You can acknowledge, "I'm having the thought, 'I can't do this because . . .'"
- You can ask yourself the kidnap question: "If the life of a loved one depended on it, could I attempt this goal, even with all these 'reasons' not to?"
- You can name the stories underlying the reasons: "Aha! The 'too tired' story or the 'not enough time' story."
- You can simply let these thoughts come and go like passing cars while you focus your attention on taking action.

Where to from Here?

This is a key juncture in the book. You know your values, and you've set some goals; now it's time to take action. FEAR is usually the only thing that prevents you, and now you know how to deal with it. Yet even so, you may still be resisting taking action, which is why we're now going to look at a powerful ally for overcoming resistance. It's called . . .

31

Willingness

Suppose you're climbing a mountain that has spectacular views from the top. You're halfway up when you come to a really steep slope where the path is narrow and rocky. Right about now it starts pouring rain. Now you're cold and wet; you're struggling up this steep, slippery track and your legs are getting tired and you're gasping for air. And you start thinking, "Why didn't anyone tell me it would be this tough?"

At this point you have a choice: you can turn back or keep going. If you keep going, it's not because you want to get colder and wetter and more exhausted, it's because you want the satisfaction of reaching the summit and experiencing those magnificent vistas. You're willing to endure the discomfort not because you *want* it or *enjoy* it, but because it gets between you and where you're going.

My Lack of Willingness

I first got permission from Steven Hayes to write this book back in July 2004. But I didn't start writing it until four months later. Why not? Because every time I thought about making a start, I would feel this huge surge of anxiety: a fist-sized knot in my stomach, a tightness in my chest, and an urge to stay as far away as possible from my computer. Thoughts would flow through my head: "You're wasting your time—you'll never get published," "You don't even know how to write," "It'll just be a load of rubbish." (One particularly troublesome thought was actually a fact:

I had already written five books, each of which had taken a huge amount of time and effort and none of which had ever seen print.) Unfortunately, I fused with all those thoughts and avoided all those feelings and, as a result, I didn't write a word.

But the more I put off writing, the more dissatisfied I felt. I distracted myself in all kinds of ways: reading, going to movies, eating chocolate. I also tried telling myself, "There's no hurry. I've got the whole rest of my life to write it." But my dissatisfaction continued to grow. I was all too aware that my demons were in charge of the boat, and I felt like a total hypocrite.

Finally, after four months of growing frustration, I thought to myself, "You've got all these terrific tools and techniques. You use them with your clients every day and get great results. How about putting into practice what you preach?" So I sat down and wrote, "What is my goal?" And I answered, "To write a self-help book based on ACT." Next, I wrote, "What are the values underlying my goal?" And I answered, "The underlying values are: challenging myself, personal growth through facing my fears, helping people (after all, this book could help a lot more people than I ever could through one-on-one therapy), supporting my family (because if this book makes money, my family prospers), modeling for others the principles that I advocate (i.e., practicing what I preach), developing my career, and the creativity of the writing process itself."

Writing all this down made a huge difference. It clarified for me that not only would this book benefit others, it would also benefit me. And even if it never got published, I would learn and grow simply through the act of writing it.

Next I wrote, "What thoughts, feelings, sensations, and urges am I willing to have in order to complete this goal?" This is a very important question, which we need to ask ourselves repeatedly when facing life's challenges. And although we've already discussed it earlier in the book, it's important to really clarify the word "willingness." Willingness doesn't mean you like, want, enjoy, desire, or approve of something. Willingness means you'll allow it, make room for it, or let it be in order to do something that you value.

If I said, "How'd you like a course of injections that will make all your hair fall out and make you vomit repeatedly?" I'm sure you'd say, "No way!" But if you had cancer and I offered you a course of chemotherapy that could totally cure it, you'd take it willingly and side effects be damned. Why would you put yourself through all that? Not because you *like* or *want* or *approve of* vomiting and losing your hair. No, you'd take it in order to keep on doing something that you value: *living*!

Willingness means we make room for the negative side effects, such as unpleasant thoughts and feelings, in order to create a meaningful life. (And luckily this, in turn, gives us plenty of positive side effects.) But willingness doesn't mean merely tolerating, gritting our teeth, or being able to stand it. It means actively embracing our experience, even though we don't like it.

Suppose you're in a loving, committed relationship and your partner wants to invite his or her father over for dinner. And suppose you intensely dislike your partner's father. You dislike his dress sense. You dislike his aftershave. You dislike his opinions, his boastfulness, and his arrogance. Yet inviting this man for dinner would mean the world to your partner. If it's really important for you to support your partner, then you could invite this man over for dinner, greet him warmly at the door, welcome him into your house, and make him feel completely at home, even though you intensely dislike him. That's willingness.

Willingness in Everyday Life

Willingness is something we practice in small ways every day of our lives. For example, when you go to the movies, you're willing to pay for the ticket. It's not that you actively want to pay for it. If someone said, "Here's a free ticket," you wouldn't say, "No, thanks. I really prefer to pay my hard-earned money for that ticket." So it's not that you like paying for that ticket. It's more that you consent to pay for it in the interest of seeing the movie. Similarly, if you're going on vacation, you probably don't enjoy packing your suitcases. You don't desire it, but you go ahead and do it in the interest of having a good trip.

Willingness is essential because it's the only effective way to deal with life's obstacles. Whenever an obstacle presents itself, you can either say yes or no. If you say no, your life stagnates or shrinks. If you say yes, your life gets bigger. If you keep saying yes, there's no guarantee life will get easier, because the next obstacle may be just as difficult or even tougher. But saying yes becomes more of a habit, and the experience you gain from this gives you a reservoir of strength.

Even if you don't *want* to say yes, you can still *choose* to. And each time you make that choice, you grow as a person.

At the same time, the more you practice expansion and defusion, the less discomfort you actually have to deal with. If you see the thought, "You'll fail" as only words, it's a lot easier to accept it. And when you turn off that struggle switch, your feelings are a lot easier to live with because they don't get amplified.

When the struggle switch is ON, you do whatever you can to avoid or get rid of uncomfortable feelings. But when it's OFF, you simply allow them to be. In other words, you are *willing* to have them, even though you may not *want* them.

Willingness Has No Shades of Gray

Willingness is an all-or-nothing experience, like being pregnant or being alive. Either you're willing or you're not. There's no in-between. This all-or-nothing property of willingness is expressed in the ancient Eastern saying: "You can't leap a chasm in two jumps."

To pursue her goal of finding a partner, Soula joined a commercial dating agency. She was willing to make room for feelings of vulnerability, insecurity, anxiety, and for thoughts like "I'm wasting my money," "I'll meet only weirdos and losers," and "If I do meet anyone nice, they won't like me." Her willingness enabled her to go on some dates and meet some nice guys.

To spend more quality time with her children, Michelle was willing to have the anxiety of repeatedly saying no to her boss's extra-work demands.

To reclaim her life and put her alcoholism behind her, Donna was willing to grieve for her husband and child—to let her sadness be there—without trying to drink it away.

Kirk was a commercial lawyer who realized, once he had connected with his values, that his work was not meaningful. He had become a lawyer primarily for status and money and also to win the approval of his parents (who were both lawyers). What he really wanted to do, though, was to support and care for people, and especially to help them grow, learn, and develop. Ultimately, he decided to retrain as a psychologist. In order to do this, he was willing to make room for a lot of discomfort: loss of income, many years of extra study, parental disapproval, anxiety over whether he was doing the right thing, thoughts about "all those years wasted," and so on. The last time I saw Kirk, he'd graduated as a psychologist and loved the profession. But he'd never have gotten there without willingness to make room for that discomfort.

My Willingness

So now let's return to how I wrote this book. As mentioned above, my next step in overcoming my inertia was to write down all the thoughts, feelings, sensations, and urges that I would be willing to have in order to achieve my goal. My thoughts included, "It's too hard," "I can't write," "I'm wasting my time," and "I'll never get published." My feelings included anxiety, boredom, and frustration. My sensations included a tightness in my jaw, churning in the stomach, sweaty palms, and a racing heart. And last but not least, I had strong urges to run away, play with the dog, go to sleep, get something to eat or drink, read a book, look up words in the dictionary, surf the Internet, watch television, or do anything else except write!

Writing this down was enormously useful because it helped me take a realistic look at the situation: to prepare for the demons I'd be facing on my voyage. That way, there would be no surprises.

Next I wrote, "Is there any one of these thoughts and feelings that I can't handle, provided I practice expansion and defusion?" And the answer I wrote was: "No. Provided I defuse these thoughts and make room for these feelings, I can handle every one of them."

The next question was, "What would be useful to remind myself?" In answer to this, I pulled out a blank card and wrote down three inspiring quotes:

"A journey of a thousand miles begins with one step."
—Lao Tzu

"The first draft of anything is shit!"

—Ernest Hemingway

"Twenty years from now you will be more disappointed by the things that you didn't do than by the ones you did do. So throw off the bowlines. Sail away from the safe harbour. Catch the trade winds in your sails. Explore. Dream. Discover."

—Mark Twain

Obviously, these quotes apply to any meaningful enterprise, not just writing. I find them both reassuring and inspiring. And ever since that day, I've kept that card beside my computer and I frequently reread it.

Following that, I wrote, "How can I break this goal down into smaller steps?" My answer was: "I only need to write one chapter at a time. Actually, I only need to write one paragraph at a time. Come to think of it, I only need to write one sentence at a time." Once I realized that I only needed to write one sentence at a time, my anxiety lessened considerably. To write a book, that's overwhelming. But to write a sentence, that's a lot easier.

Next I wrote, "What's the smallest, easiest step I can begin with?" And I answered: "Write one sentence." Finally I asked, "When will I take that first step?" And I answered: "Right now!"

So there and then, I forced myself to start writing. The knot in my stomach was huge. So I studied it as if I were a scientist. It felt like a lump that started just above my waist and reached up underneath my rib cage. I observed it, breathed into it, and made room for it. I reminded myself, "This is nothing more than an unpleasant sensation, coupled with an urge to run away." And I asked myself, "Am I willing to have this in order to pursue my goal?" The answer came back loud and clear: "Yes!"

Then I turned my attention to the thoughts swirling around in my head: Radio Doom and Gloom playing at full volume. I pictured those thoughts as words on a television screen. I looked at them and saw them for what they were: words and pictures. Then I let them come and go while I focused on my writing.

It took me many hundreds of hours to write this book, and I had many unpleasant thoughts and feelings during that time. I've also had enormous satisfaction from acting in accordance with my values. And I've also had plenty of extremely pleasant thoughts and feelings every time I completed a paragraph, every time I completed a chapter, every time I sat down and wrote even though I didn't feel like it.

Of course, I still have no idea whether this book will ever be successful, but no matter what happens, I've gained enormously in writing it. I've developed my writing skills, learned how to simplify concepts in order to teach them more effectively, developed new ideas to enhance my work, proved to myself that ACT really works (when I remember to apply it), and had the satisfaction of living by my values. It's been vastly more fulfilling than the four months I spent avoiding writing.

Now imagine how different it would have been if my only purpose in writing this book was to become rich and famous: there would be no satisfaction or fulfillment until that goal was achieved. And because that particular outcome is so unlikely, if that were my only motivation I probably would have given up long ago.

Putting It Down in Black and White

Again and again throughout this book I've emphasized the importance of writing to clarify your thoughts, to aid conscious memory, to enhance motivation. When you set your values and goals down in black and white, you're far likelier to follow through on them. So I recommend that you write out an action plan, following the steps below, to help you achieve any goal that you're currently procrastinating on.

THE WILLINGNESS-AND-ACTION PLAN

Write out your answers to the following questions. (You can download a free plan form at the resources page on www.thehappinesstrap.com.)

1. My goal is to . . .
2. The values underlying my goal are . . .
3. The thoughts, feelings, sensations, and urges I'm willing to have in order to achieve this goal are . . .

4. It would be useful to remind myself that . . .
5. I can break this goal down into smaller steps, such as . . .
6. The smallest, easiest step I can begin with is . . .
7. The time, day, and date that I will take that first step, is . . .

As you can see, willingness is tremendously important. But by itself it's not enough for a meaningful life. There's one final piece to this puzzle, a piece that completes the whole picture, and enables you to keep moving . . .

32

Onward and Upward

No matter how well you learn to walk, sooner or later you will stumble. Sometimes you'll catch yourself in time, and sometimes you'll fall over. Sometimes you may even hurt yourself. The fact is, from the day you took your very first step, you have fallen down many hundreds of times—and yet at no point did you ever give up walking! You always picked yourself up, learned from the experience, and carried on. It is this sort of attitude that we are referring to when we use the word "commitment" in Acceptance and Commitment Therapy. You can accept your thoughts and feelings, be psychologically present, and connect with your values all you like, but without the commitment to take effective action, you won't create a rich and meaningful life. This, then, is the final piece of the puzzle—the piece that completes the whole picture.

"Commitment," like "acceptance," is a frequently misunderstood term. Commitment isn't about being perfect, always following through, or never going astray. "Commitment" means that when you do (inevitably) stumble or get off track, you pick yourself up, find your bearings, and carry on in the direction you want to go.

This is well exemplified in the legend of the great Scottish hero Robert the Bruce. It's a true story that happened seven hundred years ago, in a period of history when the king of England ruled over Scotland. The English king was violent and cruel, and he brutally oppressed the Scots for many years. But in the year 1306, Robert the Bruce was crowned king of Scotland, and he made it his number-one priority to liberate his country. Soon after he took the throne, he raised an army and led it into war against the English on the blood-soaked battlefield of Strath-Fillan. Unfortunately, the English army had greater numbers and superior weapons, and the Scots were harshly defeated.

Robert the Bruce escaped and went into hiding in a cave. Cold, wet, exhausted, and bleeding from his wounds, he felt utterly hopeless. So great was his shame, so crushing his despair, he thought about leaving the country and never returning.

But as he lay there, he looked up and noticed a spider, which was trying to spin a web across a gap in the wall of the cave. This was no easy task. The spider would spin a strand and string it from one side of the gap to the other. Then it would spin another and another, weaving back and forth to build the web. Yet every few minutes a strong gust of wind would blow through the gap, breaking the web and sending the spider tumbling.

But the spider didn't give up. The moment the wind died down, it would crawl back up to the edge of the gap and start spinning again from scratch.

Again and again the wind blew the web apart, and again and again the spider started rebuilding. Eventually, the wind died down long enough for the spider to spin a truly firm foundation, so that the next time the wind kicked up, the web was strong enough to withstand it, and the spider was finally able to finish the job.

Robert the Bruce was amazed by this spider's persistence. He thought, "If that tiny creature can persist despite all those setbacks, then so can I!" The spider became his personal symbol of inspiration and he coined the famous motto: "If at first you don't succeed, try, try again." After his wounds had healed, he raised another army and continued to battle against the English for the next eight years, finally defeating them in 1314 at the Battle of Bannockburn—a battle in which his own men were outnumbered ten to one!

Of course, Robert the Bruce didn't know he would succeed at his goal. He only knew that freedom was everything to him. And as long as he pursued that freedom, he was living a life he valued. (And he was therefore *willing* to endure all the hardship that went with it.) Such is the nature of commitment: you can never know in advance whether you will achieve your goals; all you can do is keep moving forward in a valued direction. The future is not in your control. What is in your control is your ability to continue your journey, step by step, learning and growing as you progress—and getting back on track whenever you wander. In the words of the great leader, Sir Winston Churchill: "Success is not final. Failure is not fatal. It is the courage to continue that counts."

Redefining Success

There's a potential danger in telling inspirational stories, such as that of Robert the Bruce. The danger is in the way we define success. Whether we're talking of artists, doctors, athletes, businesspeople, rock stars, politicians, or police officers, "successful people" are typically defined in terms of the goals they've achieved. If we buy into this woefully limited definition, then we're condemned to a goal-focused life: chronic frustration punctuated by fleeting moments of gratification. So I invite you now to consider a new definition: success in life means living by your values.

Adopting this definition means you can be successful right now, whether or not you've achieved your major goals. Fulfillment is here, in this moment, anytime you act in line with your values. And you are free from the need for other people's approval. You don't need someone to tell you that you've "made it." You don't need someone to confirm that you're "doing the right thing." You know when you're acting on your values and that's enough.

Soula, Donna, and the other people we've met in this book weren't heroes of the sort we find in movies. They didn't accomplish awe-inspiring feats or triumph against overwhelming odds. But they were all successful in connecting with their hearts and making meaningful changes in their lives. (Of course, as I've said before, living by your values doesn't mean giving up on your goals; it merely means shifting the emphasis, so life becomes about appreciating what you have now rather than always focusing on what you don't have.)

It's also worth mentioning that every one of the clients I've written about did, on many occasions, go "off track." They all lost touch with their values at times, got caught up in unhelpful thoughts, struggled with painful feelings, and acted out in self-defeating ways. But because they were committed, sooner or later they always got back on track again.

Take Donna, for example. It took her the best part of a year to recover completely from her alcoholism. There were plenty of times where she stayed off the drink for a few weeks, but then something would trigger another binge: the anniversary of the car crash, the anniversary of the funeral, the first Christmas Day since her husband and daughter had died. Occasions such as these brought up many painful feelings and memories for Donna and with them came strong urges to drink. At times she "forgot" all the skills she'd learned in therapy and turned to alcohol to try to escape her pain.

But as time went on, Donna got better and better at catching herself. Her first relapse came on the day of her daughter's birthday. This triggered an entire week of heavy drinking. Her second relapse involved only three days of drinking, and her third lasted for just one day.

Donna learned quickly that there's no point in beating yourself up when you screw up or fail to follow through. Guilt trips and self-criticism don't motivate you to make meaningful changes; they just keep you stuck, dwelling on the past. So after each relapse, Donna came back to the basic ACT formula:

> A = Accept your thoughts and feelings *and be present.*
> C = Connect with your values.
> T = Take effective action.

So what does this mean in practice? Well, the first step, once you've gone off track, is to recognize it consciously, to be fully present with what's happening. At the same time, you need to accept that once this has happened, you can't change it; there is no way you can possibly alter the past. And while it may be valuable to reflect on the past and think about what you might do differently next time around, there's no point in dwelling on it and crucifying yourself for being imperfect. So accept that you went off track, accept that it's in the past and is now unchangeable, and accept that you're human and therefore imperfect.

The second step is to ask yourself, "What do I want to do now? Rather than dwelling on the past, what can I do in the present that's important or meaningful?"

Then the third step is, of course, to take committed action in line with that value.

Try, Try Again?

Robert the Bruce's motto, "If at first you don't succeed, try, try again" is certainly powerful, but it's only half the story. The other half of the story is that we must assess whether what we're doing is effective. A better motto might be: "If at first you don't succeed, try, try again; and if it still isn't working, try something different."

But there's a fine line to tread here, too. Whenever you face a signif icant challenge, the "It's too hard!" demons will be on your back. "You can't do it! Give up!" your mind will tell you. And the temptation then is to quit and try something else. Yet, often persistence is precisely what is required. In the words of the great inventor Thomas Edison: "Many of life's failures are people who did not realize how close they were to success when they gave up." This is where your mindfulness skills come in handy. By paying full attention to what you are doing and noticing the impact it is having, you're in the best position to answer this question: "In order to achieve my goals, do I need to persist with my behavior or change it?" Then, depending on your answer, commit to either changing that behavior, or persisting with it.

An Attitude of Optimism

As we saw in the last chapter, Soula joined a dating agency and started going out with a variety of different men. At first this was an awkward, embarrassing, and nerve-racking process for her. Her mind repeatedly told her she was a "loser" and that she would only ever meet other losers. But despite these unhelpful stories, Soula persisted, and over time she gradually became more comfortable with the process.

Some of her dates were disastrous: the men were boring, arrogant, sexist, egotistical, or just generally obnoxious. On the other hand, some of her dates were a lot of fun: the men were witty, charming, intelligent, open-minded, and attractive. It was always hit-and-miss. At one point she dated a guy for seven weeks, fell madly in love with him, and then found out he'd been cheating on her. Naturally, she was devastated and, being human, she went off track for a while. For over a month she fell back into her old habits: staying home alone, cutting herself off from friends, dwelling obsessively on her loneliness, and eating ice cream by the bucket to "cheer herself up." Still, eventually Soula realized what she was doing, and she applied the basic ACT formula.

As a first step, she made room for her sadness and her loneliness. She defused from her story that "life is worthless without a partner," and she chose to connect with the present (instead of stewing pointlessly over the past). Second, she connected with her values: her desire to cultivate loving, meaningful relationships. Third, she took effective action: she resumed spending time with friends and family, and she also continued the dating process.

A little while later Soula fell in love with another man, whom she dated for over seven months. Unfortunately, it didn't work out; they split up because Soula wanted to get engaged but he wasn't ready to settle down.

So far, there's no fairy-tale ending to Soula's story. The last time I saw her, she was still dating. But she was also investing in meaningful, loving relationships with her friends and family and herself—and although this didn't get rid of her desire for a partner, it certainly gave her a lot of satisfaction and fulfillment. What's more, she had developed a sense of humor about the dating game. She had learned to see it as an opportunity to meet new people, discover new social venues, and learn more about men! She also used dates as an opportunity to try new activities, from playing miniature golf to riding horses. In other words, the process of dating became a valued activity: a means for personal growth rather than a painful ordeal driven by loneliness.

As we go through life, we encounter all sorts of obstacles, difficulties, and challenges, and each time this happens we have a choice: we can embrace the situation as an opportunity to grow, learn, and develop, or we can fight, struggle, and try whatever we can to avoid it. A stressful job, a physical illness, a failed relationship: all these are opportunities to grow as a person, to develop new and better skills for dealing with life's problems. As Winston Churchill put it: "A pessimist sees the difficulty in every opportunity; an optimist sees the opportunity in every difficulty."

ACT is an inherently optimistic approach. ACT assumes that no matter what problems you encounter, you can learn and grow from them; no matter how dire your circumstances, you can always gain fulfillment from living by your values; and no matter how many times you wander off the path, you can always get back on track and start again, right where you are.

Choose to Grow

A core theme in this book is that life involves pain. Sooner or later we all experience it—physically, emotionally, and psychologically. But in every painful life circumstance there is an opportunity for us to grow. Earlier in the book we encountered Roxy, a thirty-two-year-old lawyer who had been diagnosed with MS (multiple sclerosis). Before her illness, Roxy's life had been totally focused on work. Success in her career meant everything, and she had done very well for herself, getting promoted to junior partner and earning a huge salary. But she was working an average of eighty hours a week, lived on takeout food, rarely exercised, and was always "too tired" to spend time with friends and family. Her relationships with men were typically short-lived because she never had the time or energy to invest in them. And she rarely found time to chill out and have fun.

Facing the possibility of severe disability or premature death awoke Roxy to the fact that there's more to life than work and money. She realized that our time on this planet is limited, and she connected with what was most important, deep in her heart. She cut back on her work hours, spent more time with the people she cared about, and began to look after her health through swimming, yoga, and sensible eating.

She also changed the way she related to people at work. She had always been so driven to excel, she'd paid little attention to social niceties in the workplace and, as a result, appeared to her colleagues as closed-off and cold. Now she started treating her colleagues differently, showing an interest in their lives outside work and opening up, letting them know more about her own life. As she warmed to her colleagues, they in turn warmed to her, and she started to make some genuine workplace friendships.

By embracing the opportunity in her difficulty, Roxy made her life far richer and more meaningful. Of course, she would rather not have had the illness in the first place, but since that was not in her control, she chose to go down the path of personal growth.

Stories like this are commonplace. I have seen many people face a serious diagnosis—cancer, heart disease, a stroke—and completely re-evaluate their lives as a result. But we don't have to wait until death is looking us in the eyes; we can make meaningful changes whenever we wish. And the more we do so, the more effectively we create . . .

33

A Meaningful Life

So here we are at last: the final chapter. Hopefully, by this stage, your psychological flexibility has improved and you're already creating a rich and meaningful life. If that's you, carry on; do more of what's working. But if it's not happening, you need to look at why it isn't and what you can do about it. However, before we go any further, let's recap the six core principles of ACT:

1. DEFUSION
   Recognizing thoughts, images, and memories for what they are—just words and pictures—and allowing them to come and go as they please, without fighting them, running from them, or giving them more attention than they deserve.

2. EXPANSION
   Making room for feelings, sensations, and urges and allowing them to come and go as they please, without fighting them, running from them, or giving them undue attention.

3. CONNECTION
   Bringing full awareness to your here-and-now experience with openness, interest, and receptiveness; focusing on and engaging fully in whatever you're doing.

4. THE OBSERVING SELF

A transcendent part of you; a perspective from which to observe difficult thoughts and feelings, without being hurt by them. The one part of you which is unchanging, ever-present, and impervious to harm. It has no physical properties: it is "pure awareness."

5. VALUES

Clarifying what is most important in your heart: what sort of person you want to be, what is significant and meaningful to you, what you want to stand for in this life.

6. COMMITTED ACTION

Taking effective action in line with your values (again and again, no matter how many times you go off track).

These six basic principles are neatly summarized in the basic ACT formula:

A = Accept your thoughts and feelings *and be present*.
C = Connect with your values.
T = Take effective action.

The more you live by these six core principles, the more fulfilling and rewarding your life will be. But don't believe this just because I say so. Try it out and trust your own experience. If these principles work for you, if they give you a rich, full life, then it makes sense to embrace them as fully as possible.

At the same time, see this as a personal choice. You don't have to live by these principles. There's no obligation, no right or wrong, good or bad. If you embrace these principles, it won't make you a "good person" or superior to others in any way. And if you ignore them, it won't make you "bad" or "inferior." If you go around thinking you have to live by these principles, it creates a sense of coercion, as if you were being forced to do something you don't really want to do—and that's neither pleasant nor constructive. Such an attitude only gives rise to pressure, stress, and anxiety and ultimately leads to failure.

The way you live your life is a personal choice. And while most people find that these six basic principles will transform their lives in many positive ways, it's important to remember they aren't the Ten Commandments! Apply them if and when you choose to, and always in the interest of making life richer, fuller, and more meaningful. But don't make them into rules that must be obeyed absolutely and at all times!

I'm quite sure there will be plenty of times when you "forget" what you've learned in this book. You'll get caught up in unhelpful thoughts, struggle uselessly with your feelings, and act in self-defeating ways. But the instant you recognize what you're doing, you can choose to do something about it—if you want to, that is. Again, this is a personal choice. You don't *have* to do anything. In fact, I'm sure there will be times that you deliberately choose not to use the principles in this book. And that's okay. Just aim to be more aware of the choices you make and the effects they have on your life. That way, you are more likely to make choices that enhance your life, rather than ones that diminish it.

Feeling Stuck?

It may be that you've reached this point in the book and still haven't made many (or any) significant changes. If that's what's happening, you've probably come up against one or more components of FEAR:

> Fusion.
> Excessive expectations.
> Avoidance of discomfort.
> Remoteness from values.

So if you're feeling stuck or you're putting off taking action, take a few moments to identify what's getting in your way and think about how to resolve it. If you're fusing with unhelpful thoughts such as, "It's too hard," "I can't do it," "It won't work," "I can't be bothered," "I'll do it later," then practice defusion skills. If your expectations are unrealistic, break your goals down into smaller steps, give yourself more time, and allow yourself to make mistakes. If you're avoiding uncomfortable feelings such as fear or anxiety, practice your expansion skills and develop willingness. If you're remote from your values, then keep asking yourself, "What do I really care about?" "What really matters deep in my heart?" "What sort of person do I want to be?" "Deep down inside, what do I really want?"

And if you're not quite sure how to implement these solutions, then go back to the relevant chapters in the book. This book was never intended to be read just once and integrated fully into your life. It's intended to be used as a reference book. As often as you need to, go back to the relevant chapters and read them again. (*And if you've read through the book without doing any of the exercises, now's the time to go back and actually do them!*)

Applying ACT in Different Domains of Life

In whichever domain of life you feel dissatisfied—whether it's health, work, friends, family, relationships, or something else—applying the basic ACT principles will help you transform it. Whatever you're doing, engage yourself fully in it. Whoever you're with, be present. When unhelpful thoughts arise, defuse them. When unpleasant feelings arise, make room for them. And whatever your values are, be faithful to them.

Using the six core principles of ACT can help you rise to the Serenity Challenge: "Develop the courage to solve those problems that can be solved, the serenity to accept those problems that can't be solved, and the wisdom to know the difference." If your problems *can* be solved, then take effective action, guided by your values, to solve them. If your problems *can't* be solved, use defusion and expansion to accept this. And the more awareness you bring to your experience right now—the more you'll be able to tell which problems are which.

No matter what sort of problematic situation you encounter in life, there are only ever two sensible courses of action:

1. Accept it.
2. Take effective action to improve it.

Of course, sometimes the only way to improve the situation is to leave it. But if you can't leave it and if no effective action is possible *right now*, then the only option is to accept it until you *can* take effective action.

Focus on What's in Your Control

Whatever you attempt to do, you'll get the best results when you focus on what is in your control (and the worst results when you focus on what's not in your control). So what *is* in your control? Well, mainly two things: your actions and your attention. You *can* control the actions you take, no matter what your thoughts and feelings may be telling you (as long as you are aware of your internal experience and you focus on what you're doing). And you *can* control how you direct your attention; that is, what you focus on and whether you do so with openness, interest, and receptiveness.

Apart from your actions and your attention, you don't have much control over anything else. For example:

- You have little control over your feelings, thoughts, memories, urges, and sensations—and the more intense they are, the less control you have.
- You have no control over other people. (You can *influence* other people, of course, but only through your actions. Therefore, those people are not *directly* in your control; only your actions are. Even if you were to point a gun at someone's head, you couldn't control them, because they could still choose to die rather than obey you.)
- You have no control over the world around you. (You can interact with and transform the world around you, but *only through your actions*—your actions are in your control; the world isn't.)

Therefore, it makes sense to put your life's energy mainly into action and attention. Do what you value. Engage yourself fully in what you're doing. And pay attention to the effect your actions are having. Remember, each time you act in line with your values, no matter how tiny that action is, you're contributing to a rich and meaningful life.

How Far Have You Come?

The whole purpose of this book is to help you escape from the vicious cycle of the happiness trap—to live a full and meaningful life instead of basing your existence on chasing "good" feelings and avoiding "bad" ones. Of course, in a full human life you will experience the full range of human feelings. You will experience every emotion, from joy and love to fear and anger, and willingly make room for them all.

So how far have you come since you started this book? How often are you still getting caught in the happiness trap—running away from "negative" emotions and desperately striving for "positive" ones? If you really want to know, try this. Turn back to the very end of chapter 1 and do the Control of Thoughts and Feelings Questionnaire (page 15) again. Compare your score now with your score when you started the book. If it's lower, then you're on the right track. If it's not, then you've still learned something valuable: that although you may have gained some useful ideas from this book, you haven't yet applied them effectively in your life. (And if that's the case, there's no need to worry—it simply means you need to do more practice.)

There's an ancient Eastern saying: "If you don't decide where you're going, you'll end up wherever you're heading." To live a meaningful life, you need direction, and your values are there, deep in your heart, to provide it. So connect with those values; use them for guidance. Cultivate a sense of purpose. Keep setting meaningful goals and pursue them vigorously. At the same time, appreciate what you have in your life right now. This is important, because now is the only time you ever have. The past doesn't exist; it's nothing more than memories in the present. And the future doesn't exist; it's nothing more than thoughts and images in the present. The only time you ever have is this moment. So make the most of it. Notice what is happening. Appreciate it in its fullness.

And remember: *life gives most to those who make the most of what life gives.*

Acknowledgments

Words cannot adequately express the enormous gratitude I feel toward Steven Hayes, the originator of Acceptance and Commitment Therapy (ACT). He has given a great gift to me, my family, my clients, and to the world at large. I am also indebted to the wider ACT community for all the useful advice, experience, and information that is so freely shared among them at workshops, conferences, and via the Internet. I am especially grateful to Kelly Wilson and Hank Robb, whose insights and interventions I have frequently drawn upon throughout these pages, and likewise to all those colleagues in the ACT community who have given me feedback and advice during various stages of writing: Jim Marchman, Joe Ciarrochi, Joe Parsons, Sonja Batten, Julian McNally, and Graham Taylor.

I would particularly like to acknowledge my brother, Genghis, who has (as always) been an inexhaustible source of advice, strength, and encouragement, especially during those dark times when I felt like giving up on the book altogether. I'd also like to thank all the friends and family who helped out by reading the book (or parts of it) and giving me feedback: Johnny Watson, Margaret Denman, Paul Dawson, Fred Wallace, and Kath Koning. And major thanks to my mother and my wife, who both helped out by typing up major chunks of the book: no easy task when working from my spidery handwritten scrawls.

I would particularly like to thank Carmel for all the useful input and feedback she has given me during the writing of this book, as well as for her ongoing support (and her willingness to put up with my prolonged periods ensconced at my computer).

Heartfelt thanks to the four editors who worked with me at various stages: Xavier Waterkeyn, who helped enormously with the early chapters and also came up with the book's title; Michael Carr, who did the major "grunt work," and taught me a lot in the process; Monica Berton who helped wonderfully in trimming the fat and pulling the Australian edition into its final shape; and Eden Steinberg, whose experience, insight, and personal knowledge of the material was invaluable when we reworked this book for the U.S. edition. And of course I am especially grateful to all the good folks at Shambhala Publications, who have worked so hard to bring this book together. And on that note, many thanks to my agent, Sammie Justesen, and also to Gareth and Benny St John Thomas, for delivering this book into the capable hands of the Shambhala team.

Last, but not least, a big thank-you to columnist and author, Martha Beck. Her article on ACT in O: *The Oprah Magazine* acted as a major source of inspiration, because it showed me how the complex concepts of ACT could be put into plain, simple English.

Suggestions for Crisis Times

Whenever we face a crisis, we find ourselves caught up in a storm of difficult thoughts and feelings. If we want to act effectively, then we can't allow that storm to carry us away, so the first thing we need to do is "drop anchor." In other words, we need to ground ourselves in the present moment. Once we've done that, we can consider our options.

The first step is to connect with your environment: notice five things you can see, five things you can hear, and five things you can touch or feel against your skin. Next, push your feet into the floor and get a sense of the ground beneath you. Feel it supporting you, taking your weight. Once you've done that, practice the Breathing to Connect exercise from page 144.

Having grounded yourself in the present, keep breathing mindfully, using your breath as an anchor to hold you steady until the emotional storm starts to quiet.

Next, take a moment to scan your body and notice what you're feeling. Find the most painful feeling, observe it, breathe into it, expand around it, and allow it to be, as in the expansion exercises in chapter 13, pages 101–5.

After that, take a step back and notice all the thoughts whirring around in your head. See if you can "name the story," as on page 44.

Finally, acknowledge to yourself: "Okay, right now this is where I am, and this is what is happening. The crisis I have to deal with is [fill in the blank]. The feelings I'm having right now are A, B, C. The thoughts I'm having right now are D, E, F. And the actions I can take to deal with this crisis effectively, are G, H, I." (To download a free crisis-coping plan that shows you how to take effective action, go to the resources page on www.thehappinesstrap.com.)

Again and again, come back to these basic steps, using them over and over until the crisis has resolved. And remember: every crisis, no matter how painful, is an opportunity to grow, to expand your psychological flexibility. So whenever you get a moment, ask yourself, "How can I grow from this? What can I learn from this? What skills, knowledge, or character strengths can I develop as a result of this?"

Further Readings and Resources

Books

Harris, Russ. *The Confidence Gap: A Guide to Overcoming Fear and Self-Doubt*. Boston: Shambhala Publications, 2011.

Hayes, Steven, and Spencer Smith. *Get Out of Your Mind and Into Your Life: The New Acceptance and Commitment Therapy*. Oakland, Calif.: New Harbinger Publications, 2005.

Kabat-Zinn, Jon. *Wherever You Go, There You Are: Mindfulness Meditation in Everyday Life*. New York: Hyperion, 1994.

Resources

The official Web site for ACT is www.contextualpsychology.org. Here you'll find a wealth of information about ACT, including a directory of ACT therapists.

A variety of free resources have been designed to be used in conjunction with this book. (Some of them are linked to specific book chapters.) They can be downloaded at no cost from the resources page at www.thehappinesstrap.com.

I have also recorded a number of CDs that can be used in conjunction with this book to help you develop mindfulness skills to enhance your psychological flexibility. You can purchase these at www.thehappinesstrap.com/books_and_CDs.

Index

Index

mindfulness (*continued*)
skills, 34–35
of the world around, 199–202
"misery zone," 77
mistakes, 204
moods, 83
morning routine, connecting with, 129
motivations
core values, 197
examining, 29
multiple sclerosis (MS), diagnosis of,
70–71, 225
musical soundtrack, 73
musical thoughts, 42–43, 45

Nazi death camps, survival in, 170, 172
negative feelings, 1, 10–11
negative thoughts. *See also* unhelpful
thoughts
are not the enemy, 61–62
defusion techniques, 70–75
demotivating, 46–47
recurring, 11, 52
unjustified, 48–49
newspaper stories, 38–39
Nietzsche, Friedrich Wilhelm, 170
Notice Five Things exercise, 129
numbing strategy, 22

observing
daily experiences, 199–202
process of, 101–2
vs. thinking, 64–65
observing self, the,
awareness of, 158–60
connection and, 125–26
in everyday life, 161–62
experiencing, 98–100
explained, 34, 228
function, 63–64

noticing yourself noticing, 158–59
"psychological space" of, 163
qualities, 146, 160–61
weather analogy, 161
obstacles. *See* difficulties
opportunities vs. difficulties, 225
opposites, attraction of, 152
optimism, attitude of, 223–24
overweight, 21, 23, 46

pain of living, 6, 24–25, 72, 104, 137
panic disorder, 88–89, 139
past, accepting, 222
perfection, 204
personal dislikes, 149
personal growth
as choice, 225–26
values related to, 176–77
physical exercise, 206–7
positive thoughts
radio analogy, 65–66
unhelpful, 61
present, being. *See* connection
present moment, 140–41
problems
common, 196
reaction to, 19
sharing, 15
solutions becoming, 19–21
vicious cycles, 19–21, 96

quicksand analogy, 86, 101
quotes, inspiring, 215–16

radio analogy, 65–66
reason-giving, 206–9
recreation, values related to, 177
reflex reactions, 82
rejection, avoiding, 4, 20, 149–50

Index

Index

About the Author

Dr. Russ Harris is a physician and psychotherapist specializing in stress management. Having used the principles of Acceptance and Commitment Therapy (ACT) to overcome his own struggles with anxiety, he now trains individuals and mental-health professionals to use the ACT techniques to overcome a range of psychological problems and improve the quality of their lives. He lives in Melbourne, Australia.

For more information about Russ's ACT workshops, which he now runs in several different countries, please visit: www.thehappinesstrap .com/workshops.

Russ also runs a variety of corporate programs based on psychological flexibility training. These programs are highly effective for reducing stress in the workplace, increasing vitality, improving performance, and enhancing leadership. If you are interested in learning more, please visit: www.psychologicalflexibility.com.